We are the Shac

WE are

the SHAC

Open your mind to see all people

Stories and (most) photographs

by debra harman miller

Graphics by STOP the MADnESS MEdia

We are the Shac

For permission requests, please email:

wearetheshac@gmail.com

Library of Congress Control Number: 2021923

ISBN 978-163625910-9   US $20.00
                           52000

9 781636 259109

On behalf of the Austin Area

Mental Health Consumers, Inc.

Board of Directors,

we hope that this book and the

wonderful people who shared

their stories will help you to know that

Recovery & Wellness

while living with

mental health challenges

is Real *and* Possible

Enjoy!

Duncan Cormie, Board Chair

Simone Pollard, Board Vice-Chair

Donna Waggoner, Member   Alisha Shipp, Member

Ru'Kaiel Johnson, Member

We Are the Shac

Austin Area Mental Health Consumers, Inc.

Hope & Recovery

SELF - HELP & ADVOCACY CENTER

WE,

*the members of
Austin Area
Mental Health Consumers, Inc.
at the SHAC, hereby dedicate our book,*

WE are the SHAC *to*

MetroAccess *Drivers & Staff*

*for the wonderful services they provide in Austin,
Texas; especially to the thousands of drivers for
their Professionalism, Kindness, Superior Service
....and Jedi parking SKILLS!*

We are the SHAC

Table of Contents

by debra harman miller

Open your mind to see all people

by de*bra* ha*rman* miller   xi

We Are the SHaC

Deb Miller & Ruby Tuesday

2015-2022

Author, WE are the SHAC

Mental Health Peer Specialist Intern

*by de*bra *harman* miller

Open your mind to see all people

Foreword

As the "handicapped" bus arrived at Austin Area Mental Health Consumers at the Self-Help and Advocacy Center on Wednesday morning, September 2, 2015, I hesitated. I did not think I would even be allowed to come inside. As I disembarked from the bus, I could clearly see what appeared to be an old Pizza Hut with the sign "Integral Care" on the left side of the building. (Integral Care is the Travis County Mental Health authority in Austin, and I resided in an assisted living apartment in Williamson County in the northwest corner of the city.)

Basically, I lived in the Bermuda Triangle of Mental Health Care in Austin, Texas at that time as I had no access to Travis County mental health services. Williamson County's Bluebonnet Trails mental health clinic stands ten miles away in the nearby City of Round Rock. It was neither within walking distance nor within Capital MetroAccess service area. At that time, I was confined to a wheelchair as a preventive measure as I was a "high fall risk," and any travel was difficult to arrange without the Special Transit Services or MetroAccess.

At first, I could not look around because all I could see was what was wrong with me. I scratched my name near the top of the membership form and dropped my pen. "Parkie fingers," I muttered to myself. (The tremors from my Parkinsonism makes it very difficult to hold onto anything.) I reached way down from the wheelchair to the floor for the pen and when I looked up, I saw the other persons in the room were also broken in such variations and combinations that I began to see myself in a new light. I was not the most hideous person in the world...

and alone.

by debra harman miller

We are the Shac

SHAC Executive Director, Ms. Shannon Carr, remembers this day vividly. Like many, I was in crisis, and I could not stop crying. I thought maybe, just maybe, if I paid the $23.25 for next month's bus pass, I could somehow stay alive long enough to use it.

Deb Miller Sept. 2, 2015

I took a short video crying and asking for help, but there was no one I felt safe to send it to....

by *debra harman miller*

Open your Mind to see all People

The first person I connected with was LaTanya Titus. She rolled up in an identical pink Quantum motorized wheelchair and was chatting away when she dropped her cell phone. I identified with her both because our chairs matched, and that even though we had different medical conditions, the symptoms created similar challenges. When she dropped her own phone, she shared her solution and advocated for me by teaching me how to obtain an Otterbox Defender case for myself.

LaTanya and the others were actually smiling, and I remember thinking.... Why are THEY happy? What IS their secret? I had not felt welcomed anywhere for a long time, as my physical symptoms were so disturbing to witness, complete strangers went out of their way to make sure I was aware of the uncontrolled facial movements related to the dystonia of Tardive Dyskinesia that I live with. I had not felt safe to go out in public for a long time due to the humiliating symptoms that often prompt callous remarks correlating my facial movements to those of an addict on meth-amphetamines. Double stigma.

--- --- ---

During orientation, Cindi Patton sat with me and shared the details of the Half-Priced Bus Pass Program, what actions I needed to take to qualify, including the dates I could pay for the next months' pass... Thursdays. And then she did something no one had done for a very long while; she invited me to come back the very next day.

As the MetroAccess driver tethered my chair and we began the 22-mile trip home from downtown, tears streamed down my face. It was suddenly clear the isolation to avoid the stares and the hurtful comments had driven me over the edge.

by debra harman miller   xv

We are the SHAC

Spending the day at the SHAC had given me a sense of worth and the confidence to reach out for help.

  That night I posted on Facebook, "Does anyone want to say goodbye? A person from my high school class of 1976 responded with a question, "Where are you going?" I typed my answer, "N O W H E R E." That one word on anti-social media may have saved my life, as it triggered three schoolmates from my hometown of Kingfisher, Oklahoma who were living in different parts of the country to reach out and call the local authorities.

  The police came to my door and awoke me and called for a mental health deputy from Travis County. When he arrived and they discovered he had no jurisdiction in WillCo, and I was not in immediate danger, they left. Later, when my best friend from Girl Scouts, Sheila, reached out from Las Vegas and offered to help find someone to care for my dogs, I accepted help and admitted myself to Austin Lakes Hospital.

  Four days later I was home with a new drawerful of pill bottles and a referral to a psychiatrist two months away who informed me they did not take new Medicare patients when I called for an appointment. I had hit a brick wall again. Left with no other persons I felt safe to talk to about my mental health, I called and made a reservation with MetroAccess to return to the SHAC the next day.

by debra harman miller

When they adjusted my meds, I had resolved to take better care of myself and serendipitously, the first class that day was the WRAP© class led by Certified Mental Health Peer Specialist, Mr. Donald Seamster. In the WRAP© class, we share the details of our daily routine when things are going well. Practicing the WRAP© is well-documented by SAMSHA as the most effective tool used in achieving mental health recovery and maintaining mental health wellness today. Sticking to our daily routine in our personal wellness plan gives us the freedom to stay focused and to make deliberate choices that help us achieve our "Human Potential." The WRAP© is discussed more fully in the personal stories that follow.

WE are the SHAC has taken far longer to complete than I could have ever anticipated. I had to reboot my life several times as I had six major surgeries and was injured when a car struck my motorized wheelchair as I crossed the street in my neighborhood. **However, one of the benefits of this lengthy process is that by 2018, the quality of the photographs improved dramatically as my tremors became more manageable.**

I also wish to thank those volunteers who submitted their photographs electronically, (mostly selfies,) during the pandemic shutdown. **Although they also may appear blurry in the 2020-21 check ins; they also have significance as they are indicative of the extended isolation our high-risk members faced.**

--- --- ---

Instead of giving up, I was even more determined that I start again. At first, I thought maybe the only reason I DID survive was that I was destined to finish this book. The person I consider my spiritual advisor, gave me comfort by sharing a message to wait, *that it was just not time. Something was missing and that it would be revealed to me....*

As I wrote and re-wrote these stories

over the past six years,

it was clear that I certainly wasn't

at a loss for words.

They just came out plain ole

M E A N !

In fact, what has been the greatest challenge in writing WE are the SHAC: eliminating my own stigmatizing words and **Able-ist** language. So many seemingly innocuous, familiar words have become a form of dismissive shorthand used to shame and manipulate ordinary persons by comparing one or more of their human characteristics to the symptoms of a severe mental

by debra harman miller

illness. The task was to OPEN my OWN mind that I might see all people and to share their stories without trying to judge and label them. As I wrote and rewrote this book in twelve- to eighteen-month intervals over the past six years, weaving in and out of six surgeries during this period; my vocabulary grew with my understanding.

> *Ableist* language
>
> *can be just as hurtful and oppressive as the hate speech against any other minority.*

I began participating in the Job Readiness Program at the SHAC as volunteer in 2016. When my best friend shared, they

We are the Shac

were shorthanded in the office around Christmas of 2019, I thought maybe I could help for a few days but felt I had too many health problems to make any formal commitment. Life is much too short when lived sandwiched between hospitalizations.

Soon, AAMHC Office Manager Ms. Rita Barnes asked me to commit to three days a week and I was brought in as a Volunteer Resource Director, which I loved. When AAMHC received a small grant that allowed them to create a position for a paid receptionist, I applied and was tested. Executive Director Ms. Shannon Carr offered me a parttime temporary position as a receptionist, which amused my specialists at Baylor College of Medicine Parkinson's and Movement Disorder Clinic in Houston greatly as they treated my uncontrolled facial movements... **until they remembered everyone must wear a mask to work.**

At first, I was not even going to apply to stay at the Front Desk Operator position, but Ms. Rita encouraged me. With the money I had earned as a temp, I traveled to Houston and the specialists at BCM offered me treatments of BOTOX injections placed under my jaw for my Tardive Dyskinesia that minimized the symptoms and reduced my paranoia about going out in public.

Serving as a temporary Front Desk Operator prepared me for the paid office position from June 2020 to July of 2021. In December of 2020, Ms. Shannon suggested I attended Via Hope's training and become certified as a Mental Health Peer Specialist and that AAMHC would support me in my training and supervise my internship afterward.

Via Hope was designing their online training program and I was excited at the opportunity.

by debra harman miller

My first day as Front Desk Operator, Deb Miller

In the General Support group, we support our peers who may have an opposing view of events by actively listening and respecting the variety of ways individual members experience the events.

Often persons with mental health and physical challenges share they feel like passengers in their own lives. Due to the medications many of us at the SHAC have been on, other persons have stepped up and made decisions in our best interest, which often boils down to how to meet the individual's needs efficiently and to provide convenient ways to manage their own wellness so they may meet the overwhelming demands of caring for another. It is my firm belief, as well as my personal experience, that with the strong medications some of us have L I V E D on, if a person shows up at the SHAC on the right day with their shoes tied, they are secretly a genius.

by debra harman miller

We are the SHAC

As I continued to come to the SHAC and attend groups each week, my thinking improved. When I learned new coping tools and connected with others; I found I just got better. Over time, I was able to distance myself from the idea that medications were the only acceptable solution to the mental health problem.

As I learned other coping skills to manage my symptoms, my psychiatrist worked with me to reduce the number and the amount of the medications. Tapering off the benzodiazepines due to the 2016 ruling on the dangers of combining them with the opiates required to treat the physical pain from my spinal damage was a long, and painful process, but had surprising results. Removing them and the others I was allergic to, resulted in a lessening of my symptoms, and gave me the confidence to believe I, too, could make a difference at the SHAC. When I talked to my peer mentor about my past career and a life goal to publish my own book, he encouraged me to create a written proposal to AAMHC Executive Director, Ms. Shannon Carr, including the set of interview questions, and she approved the project in December of 2016.

I created a colorful flyer and a sign-up sheet. "Every person has a story and every story matters!" Please sign up to tell your story for a book about the SHAC. Volunteers for WE are the SHAC will have their own chapter with their real name and photo.

The set of 25 basic questions were designed to prompt members to share about their favorite programs at Austin Area Mental Health Consumers, Inc. and how their experiences in the groups helped them in their own mental health recovery. However, as you will read, it sparked members to share their personal history with mental health including some very emotional and traumatic events

by debra harman miller

Open your mind to see all people

as well as the individuals' creative solutions to navigate their own physical and mental health challenges.

My original intent was edification. I was amazed at the progress I had made in such a short time, and I had also witnessed the resiliency in others.

To me we were all
like the beautiful
butterfly who is
the only one
who cannot
see the beauty
of its own wings....

It sparked the idea, how empowering and affirming it could be if they had a different perspective. What if they could see themselves from the perspective of a Loving God? What if they could share their amazing regeneration with others?

How many persons just like me were **_unnecessarily isolated and sedated,_** missing all the joy life has to offer by being a good, compliant patient? How can I find and reach out to them, that they might find the new way of living with hope and purpose that I have experienced since I came to Austin in 2014?

by debra harman miller   xxiii

We are the ShaC

Before coming to the SHAC, I knew few people with a mental health diagnosis. The book and the movie, "Sybil," about a woman with multiple personalities, came out the year I graduated high school, but my parents did not allow us to go to horror movies. The media was far from kind, sensationalizing and inferring all persons clumped into this category of mental illness, Schizophrenia, unpredictable and likened to terrorists awaiting activation from a foreign source.

I found a bipolar support group in Houston in the 90s and went to a few meetings. The information I received made me never want to go to another mental health support group ever. I showed up to the hospital seeking support, only to find there was no one with bipolar disorder in attendance; just some parents.

That day I learned I could never finish anything that took over eighteen months to complete. That I would be hospitalized every two years at a minimum, but insurance would only cover 190 days for my whole lifetime, so I had better be compliant, they warned. If I am not compliant, I can be committed against my will, and it was probable I would lose my voting rights. Don't even bother applying for a life insurance policy they told me because even the life insurance companies are betting against persons with bipolar disorder because they were frequently successful at suicide ...

Eventually!

The important thing to note, is that although NONE* of that information is true in my life today, it defined me and robbed me of hope, creating a self-fulfilling prophesy.

*I would be remiss if I did not point out that Medicare coverage still has the 190-day maximum lifetime limit on inpatient hospitalization.

by debra harman miller

Open your mind to see all people

The families shared their issues and how they felt they had borne the brunt of it... the financial hardship, the sleepless nights, the constant worry, the stress, the fear, the late-night calls, the embarrassment, the disappointment, the broken dreams. Thankfully, many family members are compassionate and very supportive.

My experience is that while others express compassion and reach out in marvelous ways, it is not as healing as the true sense of belonging that takes place when a peer believes in you and is willing to trust in you.

How difficult it can be to navigate such diversity of symptoms when there is no one clear path to recovery?

As I look the history of the peer recovery movement, I understand that people have found hope and creative ways to recover from a mental health diagnosis for decades, yet somehow, I never got the message...

Recovery from mental illness is REAL *and* POSSIBLE!

by debra harman miller

We Are the Shac

And I think I know why....

As I reviewed my own experiences as a consumer of mental health services, one of the stumbling blocks for me was that I was never "allowed" to spend any time with a person with a mental health diagnosis after we had been released from inpatient care. My only exposure to others with my diagnosis was INSIDE mental hospitals and while the patients were highly symptomatic and in such extreme crisis, the protocol was heavy sedation and sometimes ECT (electric shock therapy.) By the time treatment begins to work, patients are released to reserve benefits for future needs.

So, you may ask, "Why are we talking about these persons as "CONSUMERS?" Prior to learning about the Peer Recovery Movement, my mental health services were provided to me through the county mental health system in Houston, Harris County, Texas, through the Mental Health and Mental Retardation Authority, (MHMRA.)

by debra harman miller

Open your Mind to see all people

A typical eight am appointment began with patients standing in line for the receptionist to check them in, followed with two to four hours in the waiting area. For most, the wait would continue until after the staff returned from lunch at one pm, only to be called to the back to record vitals.

The lobby was divided in half with those who were cruelly labeled with "Mental Retardation" on the left side with a few parents and their children. The right side was designated for adult patients with a "Mental Health" diagnosis. There would be over 50 patients herded like cattle into a room with about 30 chairs that were stained and sometimes wet. I found that if I engaged in a peaceful "sit-in" on the cleaner floor, I would be whisked back to the "problem patient waiting area," which held about a dozen more patients who were called into the queue more quickly to avoid an incident.

When my turn came, I would then be escorted into a tiny office wherein one of three much-overworked psychiatrists would greet me without looking up while studying my paper file. The doctor would search for my diagnostic codes, which changed frequently due to seeing different doctors each time as well as the reclassification of disorders due the American Psychiatric Association changes to diagnostic codes to communicate more effectively with insurance companies for billing.

I would stare at the bald spot on the top of his head while he found A, B, C diagnostic codes and prescribed X, Y, and Z medications. Due to the high volume of persons in need of services, they were forced to use the "cookie cutter" style of treatment with a recipe for each diagnosis. Most psychiatrists on staff were schooled in their native country and they had little understanding about the culture of the persons they treated.

by debra harman miller   xxvii

We are the ShaC

In the late 80s it was pretty much Prozac, Lithium, Thorazine, SSRIs, and anti-seizure medications for sedation and psychosis that often drove the patient to sleepwalk (or SLEEP-EAT,) looking for the refrigerator.

--- --- ---

In my case, I left the county system in 2016 when a nurse practitioner increased the sedative medication to treat the sleep walking, increasing the symptoms. When I fell and was injured sleepwalking, I was threatened with commitment to a nursing home for my "protection." When my primary care physician and neurologist weighed in, they ordered a decrease in the dosage. Due to internal problems in Williamson County, a psychiatrist who never met me signed off on the nurse practitioners' notes and was a catalyst for me to insist on a gradual tapering of the neuroleptics. When the fall resulted in back surgery; I had enough. The collateral beauty was the beginning of my healing from Parkinsonism, and I transitioned from the wheelchair to a cane.

When a particular anti-psychotic was found to have unacceptable side effects such as diabetes, uncontrolled movements such as dystonia, or tremors, the common practice was to prescribe a very similar medication with a different brand name. Although the anti-psychotics had known side effects which were life-threatening, psychiatrists had few options. Part of the protocol at that time was regular drug holidays or timeouts where no medications would be prescribed for six weeks to see if the medication was still effective and if the patient still had symptoms. This often led to correcting an earlier misdiagnosis that may have been a temporary challenge or symptomatic of another disorder such as substance use.

by debra harman miller

Open your Mind to see all People

On the basis of a patient's self-report, and less than fifteen minutes of strained questioning, the psychiatrist (or PA – physicians' assistant,) determined their patients' quality of life with disabling sedating medications which often had permanent side-effects based on a snapshot of the person's behavior and attitude. The fear of control over a person's freedom made them the **"AUTHORITY"** as they had the power to commit patients who were noncompliant to undetermined lengths of stay in state hospitals, or to discontinue services to the individual entirely.

--- --- ---

It was difficult for the psychiatrist to gage the effectiveness of a medication as persons were informed that they could be institutionalized without warning should they deviate from the doctor's prescribed ORDERS. One of the challenges is that when the medications start working, it is so temping to think they are unnecessary and to simply forget to take them.

Dosing increased and often two of the same type or even new generics of the same medication were overlapped in an effort to taper the old drug and titrate the dosage of the new medication. Most of us have drawers of half-filled medications with unacceptable side effects so we can remember which ones have been tried and when and what was the outcome. Prescribing the side effect medication for the side effects of the side effects of the anti-psychotic was acceptable practice. Not filling a prescription or refusing the medication was flagged as non-compliance and the resulting behavior was often grounds for commitment to the state hospital. Thousands of left-over pills were and are still available to the patient for intentional suicide attempts at their discretion. Options for

We are the Shac

disposing of the excess medication was not discussed or offered at the clinics. Reform was necessary to involve the patient, (CONSUMER,) in decision-making and in goal setting.

The medications were considered effective when the person stopped talking about hearing voices, but often patients just gave up talking about them.

--- --- ---

As a disabled, low-income CONSUMER of mental health-care services; much money was invested in my healthcare through prescription medications. The goal of treatment was to eliminate symptoms that were disturbing to others and to protect me from life inside an institution. What a blessing to live in this new era wherein prescription medications support recovery from mental health challenges.

When I was released from my first inpatient treatment, in 1995, I had already spent 63 days in a 30-day treatment program at a private hospital. I was 37 at the time, so Medicare allotted me an average of a total of four days a year until I turned 65. Much reform is still needed to allow persons to get help to relieve their suffering.

When I was released, I was warned, "Don't go fishing in a toxic pond," for friendship with anyone I met there. The message was clear... You and people like you are not to be trusted and are not worthy of friendship, **even with each other.**

--- --- ---

While I was inside, I had met another patient who taught computer programming at the college. He was a former police *officer who had just learned he suffered with dissociation, or "memory" problems as they would be referred to now. A week or so later, Mark called me and said he was overwhelmed at coming home from the hospital and was ready to give up. He shared he was planning to use his service revolver that was under the seat of the truck he was driving at that moment. Desperate to help, I offered to meet him back at the same hospital and be there to support him through the intake process. I believed in my heart, that if I did not show up and keep my word, the NEXT time he would not trust in me and get the help he needed.*

When I arrived, I was told the doors of the facility were closed to former patients. So...

As I scaled the six-foot wooden fence to keep my word; it suddenly occurred to me that I was actually breaking INTO a mental hospital!

Thankfully, Mental Health Peer Specialists are welcome to come in the front door today!

Originally, I came to the SHAC to save money on my bus pass; but I stayed for two reasons:

by debra harman miller   xxxi

We are the Shac

First of all, they had a support group called the "Schizo-affective" Group. The question I hoped they could help me find the answer to was this: What is it inside me that defines my personality and what part of me is my mental illness? My thinking was that if I could:

Uncover the source of the problem.
Discover a way to treat the problem, and I could then
Recover and just be happy like everyone else seemed to be.

My second reason was that I had an enormous amount of distrust of mental health service providers in general. When I was assured AAMHC is neither controlled by the county nor duty bound to report to them, for the first time since I was diagnosed with psychotic features, I heard others like me being open about their experiences. **I was finally set free to find my truth.**

As far as I could see no one was getting paid to talk to me. Every single person in my life for the nine months prior to my first day at the SHAC were either paid to listen to me or had an agenda to monitor me in some way. This paranoia only led to more issues.

When I was formally diagnosed in 1987, I studied the variety of ways mental illness presents in others. There was no "Doctor Google" for me at that time. I read everything I could find on the subject at the public library, which was not much.

My curiosity was soon replaced with self-deprecation. I internalized the codes as immutable and created a mental ranking system of the different mental health diagnoses. By my calculations, my one "saving Grace," was that although I was in the more extreme "Bipolar 1/rapid cycler" category according to my diagnosis, at least I was not S Y B I L.

*by de*br*a* h*ar*ma*n* m*i*ll*er*

Open your Mind to see all people

Schizophrenia topped my list of the worst ones to live with every time as the idea of the loss of control over my own behavior and thoughts seemed humiliating.

As the American Psychiatric Association's Diagnostic and Statistical Manual (DSM) kept reclassifying persons according to how their symptoms presented to their physicians, I totally missed the information that BiPolar1 with Schizoaffective disorder is also a form of Schizophrenia. Even when I went back to college at 50 and earned my bachelor's in PSYCHOLOGY, I still did not put it together that they were talking about me.

After years of living with mental health challenges, others report that Aha moment of self-discovery in Mental Health recovery is comforting.

I had quite the opposite reaction. When it finally sunk in, the news was not life affirming; however, the extended interviews with volunteers for WE are the SHAC had already opened my mind to see all people INSIDE as...

EXTRAordinary!

by debra harman miller

Gratitude Pages

To all the members of Austin Area Mental Health Consumers, thank you for allowing me to be part of the Self-Help and Advocacy Center these past seven years and for supporting me in my own mental health wellness recovery journey.

I am so truly honored to be part of such a diverse membership wherein the things that make us so different from each other also make us feel so same when we are together.

To the volunteers for this project, thank you for your patience and for trusting in me to tell your truth. As you shared your stories with me, I believed I was finding out some incredible information about some wonderful people; however, it was only through hearing your words about you, that I found the vocabulary to make sense of who I truly am inside.

I am so grateful for the people who believe in my recovery and who always show up for me no matter what road I go down: Don E., Ron, Sheila, Mike, Marcie, Sonya, Matthew, Rose, Cindy, Rev. Emily, Laura Ann, Ginger, and of course, my bestie, Turtle-man!

Thank you to the Bruised Apples Mentoring Program's {{{SOS}}} Source of Support group, who hold a safe space wherein I can openly discuss the additional challenges I face with mental and physical health challenges in recovery; and who carry the message that **ANY** person can recover and can be restored to...

Sane Thinking.

by debra harman miller

Open your mind to see all people

Thank you to my physical therapists, Dr. Robert Henderson and Jason Smith, who taught me physical recovery is also Limitless.

I am so grateful for the trust I have found in my relationship with my pharmacist, Jared Binstock, who empowers me in my mental health recovery by explaining how my medications work and interact with each other and how they may affect my body, so that I can make informed choices about the risks and benefits of the medications each of my specialists prescribes.

Thank you to all my favorite MetroAccess drivers... for not only introducing me to the SHAC, (Diedra Harris,) but also for carrying me and so many others out of isolation and into the community.

We are so grateful for our caregivers and attendants who have continued their services throughout the pandemic. Thank you, Roxanna, for your dedication and professionalism.

Thank you to Dr. Matthew Lynx, M.D., who was the ONLY private psychiatrist in the Austin Area who was willing to make room for new patients with little or no insurance when I decided to break free from the Williamson County mental health system.

To recover from any illness, it takes a team of supporters, but I am also blessed through everyday acts of kindness not only from friends but also the humanitarian actions of complete strangers. Thank you to you to those individuals in our community who regularly donate food, diapers, transportation, electronics, clothing and household items, medical supplies, services, and especially TIME for your generosity of spirit and anonymous gifts.

YOU DO MAKE A DIFFERENCE in our lives!

by debra harman miller   xxxv

We are the SHAC

A special thank you to Ms. Rita Barnes and Cynthia Patton for their support and for sharing the history of the SHAC.

Thank you to Mr. Matthew Richardson for his help in editing WE are the SHAC. (Such an amazing translator of Monkey Mind!)

Also, blessings for Donald Ellerbe of Bruised Apples Mentoring Program for allowing me to be of service as a BLUE Apple, (those with physical and mental health challenges,) to co-facilitate the Bruised Apples group the past five years, and for always being willing to load up my wheelchair along with the camping gear.

And finally, thank you to Ms. Shannon Carr and the AAMHC Board of Directors for this opportunity of my lifetime, as well as your trust and patience over the past six years as I had many time outs for health issues.

When I poled each volunteer for the book, I ended the interview with one question. "If you had a magic wand, what would you give the SHAC?"

There was only ONE answer...

Their only bequest would be a bigger building so more persons could join us....

IT's just that GOOD!

Deb Miller, MHPS Intern

Wednesday FUN Day on Zoom; Christmas 2020

by debra harman miller

Part I

Introduction to:

Mental Health Peer Specialists
Via Hope
Wellness Recovery Action Plan ©
and

Welcome from our Board Chair
and our Executive Director

We are the Shac

What is a Mental Health Peer Specialist *and* WHAT DO THEY DO?

Mental Health Peer Specialists, MHPS, are persons who have lived experience with navigating their own mental health wellness and are willing to share those experiences with others. MHPS are certified on a state-by-state basis.

Certified MHPS create a *Person-Centered* environment that allows individuals with mental health challenges to make deliberate, informed choices about their lives. Peer mentorship encourages persons to set realistic goals for themselves and to find options for meeting their needs.

MHPS provide mentorship by modeling mental health recovery by practicing good self-care, sharing their lived experience with wellness tools, and by practicing wellness skills such as square breathing, meditation, and grounding. They create their own personalized Wellness Recovery Action Plan, WRAP©. Each persons' recovery journey is unique and personal and talking with others who have found creative ways to manage their own symptoms gives persons both the vocabulary and the opportunity to see themselves outside of their diagnostic label.

The certification process in Texas begins at any one of the (currently seventeen,) training entities, such as *Via Hope,* for

by d*e*br*a* h*ar*m*an* m*i*ll*er*

Mental Health Peer Specialists. Candidates must first take a self-assessment to see if they are a good match for the job duties. When the candidates feel prepared to share their lived experience with navigating mental health challenges, they commit to the training. After completing the week-long core training and fulfilling 250 supervised hours as an intern; they must file their application with the State of Texas. They are fingerprinted, and after an intensive background check, the MHPS candidates are then certified as...

Mental Health Peer Specialists.

What is Via Hope *and why are they important to persons with mental health challenges?*

Via Hope Executive Director, Dennis Bach, shares a brief history of Via Hope....

Via Hope traces its's roots to the 2003 President's New Freedom Commission which recommended transforming the nation's mental health system from a traditional medical model to a consumer, family, and youth driven recovery model; a model in which **recovery is the expected outcome for anyone with a mental health condition.**

We are the ShaC

Part of SAMHSA's response was to award Mental Health Transformation grants to eleven states, including Texas. The overall purpose was to begin developing the new infrastructure needed to support the transformed mental health system.

Via Hope was created as part of that grant in February 2009 as part of that new infrastructure. It was a joint initiative of the Department of State Health Services and the Hogg Foundation for Mental Health. *Via Hope* was initially a program housed in a partnership between Mental Health America of Texas and NAMI-Texas. In 2014, with the support and encouragement of DSHS and the Hogg Foundation, *Via Hope* became a separate 501c3 nonprofit organization which it still is today.

Prior to the pandemic in 2019, Mr. Bach reported that since that first training session for peer specialists in 2010 until the implementation of House Bill 1486 in January 2019, *Via Hope* trained 1,300 Certified Peer Specialists.

Mr. Bach shared that AAMHC Executive Director, Ms. Shannon Carr, attended the Peer Specialist Learning Community meeting on behalf of AAMHC in January of 2010. Within three months, Ms. Shannon had signed up to take part in the first group at *Via Hope* to achieve their certification as a peer specialist through the State of Texas. As a member of the Peer Run Organization Program, AAMHC has been one of "our oldest and most consistent partners." Mr. Bach adds.

Although the pandemic limited the MHPS training to a virtual platform, the curriculum was soon converted, and *Via*

by debra harman miller

Hope launched their first virtual training program. The week-long training over Zoom was a task to navigate; however, Mr. Bach shares: there was an upside, as the new MHPS candidates did not have to travel outside of Austin. Therefore, those with limited resources had a greater opportunity to attend the classes for their future certification without the added expenses of food and lodging for a week near the training site.

Our Mission

AAMHC supports and advocates for

a consumer's right to achieve

mental wellness, self-empowerment

and self-sufficiency.

by debra harman miller   5

We are the Shac

What is WRAP© and how does it Help?

The Wellness Recovery Action Plan, WRAP©, was developed by mental health professional and advocate, Mary Ellen Copeland, Ph.D., and copyrighted in 1995 by the Advocates for Human Potential.

The WRAP© is Person-Centered and begins with a Daily Maintenance plan wherein the person lists positive self-care tasks. Persons also write out a list of symptoms that may signal to the person that they are overwhelmed. The person entrusts others who agree to step in temporarily and take charge of seeing that the persons' preferences in receiving health care services are honored. Practicing the WRAP© reduces inpatient hospitalizations and empowers the person to take charge of their wellness journey.

In 2006, Copeland was presented with the United States Psychiatric Rehabilitation Association's John Beard Award for outstanding contributions to psychosocial rehabilitation. In 2009, the Substance Abuse and Mental Health Services Administration, SAMHSA, recognized the significance of Mary Ellen Copeland's contributions to mental health recovery by presenting her with SAMHSA's Lifetime Achievement Award. Information on the WRAP© has used by permission. More information is available at: **copelandcenter.com**

by debra harman miller

Chairman of the Board of Directors, Duncan Cormie, gives two thumbs up to the staff at Austin Area Mental Health Consumers, Inc. at the Self-Help & Advocacy Center for their outstanding service to members of the mental health community in Austin, Texas throughout the COVID-19 pandemic.

Duncan Cormie   2020

Austin Area Mental Health Consumers, Inc.   Board Chair

by debra harman miller   7

We are the Shac

Duncan Cormie   2020

AAMHC Board of Directors

Board Chair

As early as the 1980s, Duncan recalls hearing about Austin social services while he attended Southwestern University of Texas completing his Social Work degree. The Consumer Operated Information Network or COIN many knew served homeless in the area as the *"Drop-In Center."* Austin Travis County Integral Care (ATCIC) evolved from Mental Health and Mental Retardation (MHMR of Travis County.) The Self-Help and Advocacy Center (SHAC) building was a treasured resource for many because of the availability of showers with hot water. The *Drop-In Center* had another advantage as members could not only make free phone calls, but they could also give out the landline number so they could receive a call back.

Duncan attributes his sense of purpose and passion for helping others to the example set by his mother early on. He shares she was a "colorful person" and his inspiration. Although his family did not suffer economically, he learned to appreciate the struggles of others.

After completing his master's degree in Social Work at the University of Houston, Duncan recognized the plight of older teens who were experiencing homelessness because of the capacity limitations of children's shelters and the teens' often

by debra harman miller

intrinsic legal situations. As a social worker, he strived to make a difference for Austin youth through the nearby non-profit, *Lifeworks*. As Duncan advocated for the teens, he developed relationships within the community and was eager to learn more about Austin Area Mental Health Consumers' services. The *Lifeworks* headquarters, just down First Street, were much more spacious accommodations for private board meetings. They offered Ms. Shannon Carr, AAMHC Executive Director, the use of their conference room.

Before joining up with Austin Area Mental Health Consumers, Inc. at the Self-Help and Advocacy Center, (SHAC,) he admits he had little experience with the adult population.

In 2008, Duncan joined the AAMHC board of directors formally as a volunteer board member. Two years later, the board elected him Board Chair. Duncan continues to provide guidance and find progressive ways to serve the members throughout the pandemic and to address post crisis mental health needs in our Austin area community as they arise.

As Duncan, AAMHC Executive Director Shannon Carr, and others witnessed resiliency within the membership as they take part in support groups, they shared this dream:

We are the SHAC

VISION Statement

Our vision is to have a society wherein persons with mental health challenges are active, included, empowered, and supported by each other and the community to live strong, successful lives.

Duncan shares he has seen a "slow and steady growth in our membership." It is his experience that AAMHC at the SHAC has afforded people help and stability for recovery over the years. "The SHAC has touched a lot of lives, and the future is bright!"

He continues.... "I think that the fabric of the Austin Area Mental Health Consumers gives people the emotional support and the courage to make conscious decisions about their lives as they plan their future."

Personally, he is pleased with the diversity of support groups held at the SHAC, particularly the ones with handiwork such as *Hooked on Yarn* and the *Healing through Beading* classes.

10   *by debra harman miller*

Open your mind to see all people

Duncan shares the Board of Directors recognizes Mr. Donald Seamster, Mental Health Peer Specialist Supervisor, (MHPSS,) for the splendid work he does as a mentor both at the SHAC and throughout the Austin mental health recovery community.

The staff of Austin Area Mental Health Consumers, Inc., all have lived experience in navigating mental health wellness and Duncan is no exception. He shares a recent challenge he faced. As he was getting ready for an important meeting, he misplaced his keys. While this is not an unusual issue most ordinary persons face, as a person who is challenged with attention deficit disorder, Duncan finds that feeling of being overwhelmed manifests within him differently than the way others might experience it.

For example, an ordinary person might feel ANXIOUS when trying to remember a password. However, for a person who lives with the additional challenges of ADHD, it is more like trying to remember the password while your house is on fire, and someone is shaving the cat.

Joking aside, when we minimize a persons' disability with our casual comments to infer that a situation or a characteristic in everyday life even remotely resembles the way a person with PTSD experiences a panic attack, it is **dehumanizing.**

by debra harman miller 11

Duncan also lives with the often misunderstood, difficult to diagnose, Dysgraphia, which is not simply bad handwriting, but a separate neurological condition. Dysgraphia may have other associated symptoms such as dyslexic features, speech impairment, and is sometimes connected with the spectrum of attention deficit disorder. Dysgraphia is usually attributed to genetics; however, it can also result from trauma.

Advocate Ru'Kaiel Johnson interviews Duncan Cormie about the parking lot situation at AAMHC in December of 2020. The City of Austin protects older trees such as the one in our parking lot. The only solution would be to uproot the tree and move it to a new location, which would be very costly.

by debra harman miller

Perhaps the biggest challenge over the years, as the board supports the principle of self-determination, is finding qualified employees with lived experience to staff the office from within our membership. New funding has created opportunities for the addition of some paid positions in the office. Duncan adds that he feels the Executive Director, Ms. Shannon Carr, excels at finding workshops and training opportunities that connect and support those members who are available and interested in participating in the *Job Readiness Program* at Austin Area Mental Health Consumers, Inc. at the Self-Help & Advocacy Center.

Duncan finds the local climate of

Keep Austin Weird

allows people to feel more comfortable to

Just be Yourself!

by debra harman miller   13

We are the Shac

Ongoing, the need for a second location with adequate parking is priority. The pathway between the uneven sidewalk where members disembark from MetroAccess vehicles, and the building entrance is arduous. The large oak tree in front of the SHAC building is a protected landmark in Austin, and the only available option would be to uproot it and transplant it to a new location.

Removing the tree, leveling the parking lot, and resurfacing it has not been a practical solution because of the expense. Currently tree roots erupt through the asphalt and make the inclined and uneven surface even more treacherous to navigate as many of our members *use* mobility devices.

The COVID-19 shut down by the City of Austin has presented AAMHC with many new challenges, but for those with disabilities....

Adapting to changes in our environment is what we do best!

--- Duncan Cormie

by debra harman miller

Ms. Shannon Carr   *2017*

AAMHC Executive Director

by debra harman miller   15

We are the Shac

Ms. Shannon Carr   2017

AAMHC Executive Director

Ms. Shannon was playing on her high school volleyball team when her coach, Mrs. Wolking, signed the entire team up to serve as "HUGGERS" with Special Olympics. Confused about how hugging tied into a sporting event, she shares that experience in supporting others with special needs still guides her today. She continued volunteering her time as a trainer for Texas Special Olympics for eight years from 1988-1995. After graduating from San Marcos High School, Ms. Shannon began her degree in Social Work at Howard University.

When her mother was diagnosed with cancer, Ms. Shannon abandoned her studies to care for her. After the death of her stepmother, she tried to take on the role of matriarch.

Overwhelmed with grief and sadness, she shares it was then that the depression and anxiety she experienced crossed over from nuisance to disabling. Attempting to fill the void left by the death in her family was the catalyst for Ms. Shannon to seek professional help.

Every person on the staff at Austin Area Mental Health Consumers, Inc. has lived experience in navigating their own personal mental health challenges. Witnessing the trans-formation in the lives of their peers provides hope for the individual that recovery from mental health disability is real and possible.

In 2001, Ms. Shannon and her husband moved to Austin from Atlanta, Georgia and she applied for the coordinator's position at Texas Mental Health Consumers (TMHC.)

by debra harman miller

She was hired on the spot by then Executive Director, Mike Halligan, and she became its first paid employee. Wisely, Ms. Shannon introduced herself to everyone, worked to build relationships with the members, and took the time to listen as they shared about the issues that stand in the way of their mental health recovery. Over the years, she shares her biggest challenge was to connect Austin Area Mental Health Consumers, Inc., AAMHC, with other organizations who also offer peer support.

Nine years later, Ms. Shannon signed up for the very first *Via Hope* training for Certified Peer Specialists, registering with the State of Texas. Initially, the SHAC focused only on mental health recovery, but was later expanded to include substance use recovery peer support.

Ms. Shannon jokes that it is her nature to be a little obsessed with organization and structure; and insists upon consistency in administrative tasks based on the logistics of the projects. While the office staff jokes, "It is Shannon's way or the highway," she takes the time to explain the importance of uniformity and the reasoning behind her axioms.

As I was building an atmosphere of acceptance, I did not realize I had found acceptance also.

We are the Shac

Although she cannot participate in the discussion groups, she loves hearing the laughter as members play games and create craft items during *Wednesday FUN Day*. Her other favorite is the monthly *Meeting of the Minds*. She also loves talking to members and sharing in their *Aha-moment* of self-discovery.

> *We have people come in and say:* '*I could never put a name to what I was feeling until I came into the SHAC...*'
>
> *I love, love, love this!*

During the technical training, a wellness model was created, and the terminology shifted from stigmatizing diagnostic codes and defining labels to the *Person-Centered* approach to mental health recovery.

While in training in 2003-2004, the wellness concept of not being defined by our challenges replaced the terms such as *"I AM bipolar"* to ***"I am a person who lives with symptoms."*** Utilizing this *Person-Centered* approach, the member is empowered by discussing their shared challenges with others and learning coping tools. Wellness strategies allow persons to take an active role in decision-making. To this end, members are supported by Mental Health Peer Specialists to set and achieve realistic goals. One-to-one peer mentor sessions provide members with information about resources that may be beneficial to them. It is the role of the peer mentors as facilitators to share affirmations of self-acceptance through discussion groups as well as facilitating a variety of support groups that are "hands-on."

by debra harman miller

Ms. Shannon shares that the SHAC has always been a safe space for persons to come. Despite the lack of funding, there has always been a computer and a telephone for members to use, but the classes and the bus pass program are a result of listening to the members' challenges and creating programs to support them in achieving the goals they set for themselves.

As members recover, they look for ways to use their individual talents and skills to give back to the SHAC that has helped them so much. *Crochet with Cindy* and *Tai Chi with Thomas* are two of the classes that developed from members' desire to share their wellness tools with their peers. AAMHC at the SHAC supports those persons in their mental health recovery journey by affording them the opportunity to create new opportunities be of service. This book, for example, began with a proposal to interview volunteer members to share about their experiences at the SHAC, that Ms. Shannon approved in December of 2016. This was a long-term project and took nearly six years to come to fruition.

Texas Mental Health Consumers provided assistance for Ms. Shannon to attend training and learn business skills necessary to run the nonprofit. In addition, AAMHC at the SHAC has sponsored several persons to attend the *Via Hope* training to begin their careers as Mental Health Peer Specialists. Ms. Shannon passed the training course at *Via Hope* in 2010; later adding Mental Health Peer Specialist Supervisor to her credentials that allows her to supervise new MHPS candidates who are supported by AAMHC through the *Job Readiness Program* at the SHAC.

by debra harman miller

Surprisingly, Ms. Shannon shares she is undaunted with the opportunities to speak publicly about mental health recovery services (even when there were over 500 in attendance!)

Ms. Shannon is passionate about decreasing the disparity in providing mental health services. To this end, she is active in creating opportunities within our community to learn more about mental health recovery such as the annual Central Texas African American Family Support Conference for the past 20 years.

Advocacy and peer support are being modernized through software platforms and AAMHC plans to implement peer support management software. Ms. Shannon predicts it "will allow us to easily and readily find resources in our community and support our peers better," she sees this as a tool for greater accountability, for ourselves, the resource provider, and the person who requests the services.

"Out of our 1,300 members in our files, we have aggregated data to find the true number of persons we provide services to, and we are focusing on those folks to keep in contact with them."

NOTHING about US... WITHOUT US!

by debra harman miller

Currently, the SHAC is offering five types of peer support groups that meet live Monday thru Friday on the *Zoom* platform. Many peers are a part of these hour-long virtual classes, (including persons who live with visual challenges, who are taking part through cell phones.) The staff was eager to meet the challenge of adapting support groups, such as the seated Tai Chi class, as a virtual group to continue to be personal and interactive.

Upon reopening, the SHAC plans to continue to do "hybrid" meetings. The limited occupancy for the building translates to a maximum of 20 persons in the building (total) to comply with the mandated 25 percent rule activated by Texas Governor Abbott. The COVID-19 pandemic has made the need for a larger building even more crucial.

AAMHC would like to thank our supporters...

Via Hope

Integral Care

Amerigroup

Health and Human Services Commission of Texas

by debra harman miller

We are the ShaC

by debra harman miller

Ms. Shannon Carr   *2020-2021*

Executive Director
Mental Health Peer Specialist Supervisor

Ms. Shannon shares a lot has changed in the peer support world in the past three years. Greater recognition has been given to peer support in our community and across the nation. Ms. Shannon streamlines her time with training and meetings to increase her knowledge of business management. She is eager to take advantage of various educational opportunities in business skills, nonprofit management, and *"basically anything I can get my hands on."* She prioritizes support for her administrative staff, as well as opportunities for AAMHC Mental Health Peer Specialists and interns to train with *Via Hope* and to attend various workshops and conferences. She also keeps up with the best practices and policies in the mental health field through supporting her staff, (as well as herself,) with continuing education as a Mental Health Peer Specialist provider and Mental Health Peer Specialist Supervisor.

For the past few years, Ms. Shannon has taken great strides in making sure AAMHC is reputable and recognized for peer support, and that has made a tremendous difference in the ways we can serve our membership.

In that same realm, she adds that her priority is to "make sure that I have money in the budget to provide peer training and continued peer support." This includes certification for some, business management training and, for others, that can

We are the Shac

become the pathway to further their education in peer support and/or earning a college degree.

Ms. Shannon shares that Mental Health Peer Specialists provide the support that is a unique commodity. Peer support allows a person who is experiencing their first mental health issue or someone looking for peer support to talk to someone with shared experiences. Austin Area Mental Health Consumers at the SHAC provides members with the opportunity to talk with a peer who may have gone through the same challenges and has coped with day-to-day issues by developing wellness strategies and writing out a Daily Maintenance Plan including a personalized Wellness Toolkit utilizing the Wellness Recovery Action Plan, WRAP©*.

Ms. Shannon shares "The MHPS is a unique resource as it allows the person to find a means to keep their mental well-being and recovery strategies unique, creative and is supportive of the individual."

*Author's note: The Wellness Recovery Action Plan, WRAP©, was created by mental health professional and advocate, Mary Ellen Copeland, Ph.D., and copyrighted in 1995 by the Advocates for Human Potential. Information on the WRAP© was used by permission. More information is available at: copelandcenter.com

Via Hope is the training entity in Texas that has provided support not only for peers in the mental health field but also provides support by seeking opportunities for empowerment.

by debra harman miller

Ms. Shannon explains *Via Hope* offers a person the opportunity to not only better themselves but also to support others. *"Via Hope* has been very instrumental in providing training for professionals in the peer support industry."

When asked about her own mental health recovery journey over the past five years, Ms. Shannon describes how peer support has effected a change in her attitude regarding how she sees her part in recovery. As the airline flight attendant directs, Ms. Shannon finds she needs to put the mask on first before helping anyone else. This has even greater meaning in this time of the pandemic when our staff will mask up to greet peers.

Ms. Shannon shares "our reputation in the community has extended nationally." She fields inquiries from national organizations who are curious as to how and why AAMHC at the SHAC is so successful.

The *Half-Priced Bus Pass Program* instituted by Ms. Shannon, (like any other service at the SHAC,) started when members shared about their difficulties with paying bus fare. Ms. Shannon said the feedback was that our members were all low income, and they expressed some of their needs, which include transportation expenses. Ms. Shannon contacted Capital Metro, our local transit system, and they allowed the SHAC to join in their discount bus pass program. Discovering the needs of our members and making them a reality, "that's our job" she adds.

by debra harman miller

We are the ShaC

Previously, Ms. Shannon authored a book streamlining procedures and providing information on how Austin Area Mental Health Consumers at the Self-Help and Advocacy Center became the forerunner in mental health peer recovery, earning AAMHC the distinction of being the first such entity to qualify for Medicaid billing in the State of Texas.

Ms. Shannon shares just a few of the projects she has been a part of in our community since 2017. The Department of Human Services appointed her to the Joint Committee on Access and Forensics Services. She also was a part of the Texas Empowerment Initiative, that is an organization devoted to peer support advocacy efforts. She has taken part in the peer support recovery stakeholder meetings that bring together Peer Support Champions in the State of Texas to discuss current events and make resolutions *as one voice.* Among many, many other hats she wears, Ms. Shannon has participated in the Central Texas African American Family Support Conference for the past 20 years as a committee member, Program Chair, and currently the Conference Chair.

Currently advocacy and peer support are being modernized through software platforms and AAMHC plans to implement peer support management software. Ms. Shannon predicts it "will allow us to easily and readily find resources in our community and support our peers better." She sees this as a tool for greater accountability for our Mental Health Peer Specialists, the resource provider, and the person who requests the services.

by debra harman miller

Open your Mind to see all People

The doors to the SHAC reopened to the general membership at 100 percent capacity on July 5, 2021. With a tearful eye, many returning members shared their gratitude that they were able to rejoin their friends.

Several other members who joined the SHAC during year-long shutdown for the pandemic crisis, were excited to get to see what AAMHC looks like inside. It was also interesting to meet persons they had known virtually for a year and then get to see them in real life.

Going forward AAMHC will continue to provide services to our members. In addition, MHPS from the SHAC will expand services to the persons in the Austin Area through an outreach program funded to support patients in Austin who may be experiencing their first mental health hospitalization. MHPS provide unique support to persons who are often devasted by a confusing new diagnosis and overwhelmed. Advocating for the person to find needed resources is helpful. However, when they see their MHPS thriving; *it fosters hope that Mental Health Recovery is within their reach!*

Author's note: *As of press date, (January 2022,) the COVID-19 pandemic continues to resurface with new quarantine suggestions for our high-risk members. Most persons still attend classes over the Zoom platform, but overall attendance is up, according to Administrator, Thomas Terbay, Jr., who is responsible for data collection and group attendance verification.*

by debra harman miller   27

We are the Shac

We have reconnected with most of our pre-pandemic membership and continue reaching out to our home-bound members through the Zoom platform. In addition, members receive FUN PACKS by US mail every few months. Members share they enjoy not only the information on our peer support services, but also enjoy the Adult coloring pages of daily affirmations with wellness strategies and recovery activities.

In the Austin Community, AAMHC has earned the distinction of providing uninterrupted mental health peer support services to our membership throughout these unprecedented times. This would not have been possible without the dedication and forward thinking of Ms. Shannon Carr, MHPS Supervisor The DON Seamster, and our Board of Directors, as well as the resiliency of our individual members.

If you would like to JOIN US at the SHAC, please call, write an email, or refer a friend.

Austinmhc.org

Please focus smart phone camera on QR code on left to learn more about AAMHC, or to connect 24/7!

by debra harman miller

Part II

Programs

Austin Area Mental Health Consumers Support Services

Peer Mentor Program (One-to-One)

Information and Referrals

Half-Priced Bus Pass Program

Volunteer Program

Volunteer Appreciation Luncheon 2020 with MHPS Suzanne Edmiston Worrell, Volunteer Nancy Bible who leads the SHAC Flix Group, and Executive Director, Ms. Shannon Carr.

by debra harman miller

Job Readiness Program
MHPS Mental Health Peer Specialist Supervision Services
Computer Lab

Learning has no limits for members like Ms. Bobbie Braxton who enjoys the one-to-one tutoring sessions in the Computer Lab at AAMHC. The computer equipment updates in 2019 were made possible through a grant from the State Department of Human Services.

by debra harman miller 31

We are the Shac

AAMHC Support Groups

General Support: Monday-Friday

*Bruised Apples Mentoring Program {{{SOS}}}
Monday*

WRAP©: Tuesday

Hooked on Yarn: Tuesday

Wednesday FUN Day

General Support in Española: Thursday

Seated Tai Chi: Friday

Meeting of the Minds: 1ˢᵗ Tuesday

SHAC Snack Program: Monday-Friday

SHAC Flix: Weekly

by debra harman miller

Private pay services

AAMHC is the first Consumer Operated Service Provider (COSP) in the state of Texas to qualify for Medicaid billing.

Bruised Apples Mentoring Program, Inc.
Founded in 2003

Bruised Apples Mentoring Program began holding co-occurring disorder Source of Support Group meetings at the SHAC in 2017. Bruised Apples members; Marc Hancock, Scott C., Founder Donald Ellerbe, Judy, and co-facilitator, Joe DeFarge.

by debra harman miller 33

We are the Shac

Bruised Apples Mentoring Program's {{{SOS}}} Source of Support Group meets Mondays at the SHAC and provides information and advocacy opportunities for peer mentorship. The co-occurring disorder discussion group is led by Licensed Chemical Dependency Counselor and BAMP Founder, Donald Ellerbe, (or Don E.,) as he is known in the Austin recovery community.

BAMP links persons new in recovery who may be experiencing other related challenges with a peer who has lived experience in navigating similar obstacles while maintaining their own sobriety.

The Bruised Apples Mentoring Program comprises eleven differently colored apples representing a variety of additional challenges many face while in recovery from substance use or alcoholism. Next is a list of the colored apples and a description of each....

Bruised Apples Mentoring Program

Red Apples

Those who desire to improve their education.

Yellow Apples

Those who experience Homelessness.

by debra harman miller

Green Apples

Those involved in Recovery/Treatment and twelve-step groups.

Don Ellerbe with some of the members of the Bruised Apples {{{SOS;}}} Marcos, Ruby Tuesday & Diamond Deb, Jody Bean, Sandy Lewis, Sir Colin, and Ru' Kaiel Johnson in the fall of 2019.

Blue Apples

Those with mental or physical medical conditions.

by debra harman miller   35

We are the Shac

Brown Apples

Those with Child Protection Service Issues and/or other family issues.

Gray Apples

Those involved with, or Veterans of, the Armed Services.

Orange Apples

Those with legal issues, past or present.

Pink Apples

Those who are dealing with cancer.

Golden Apples

Those friends and families who have tried to Support US.

Rainbow Apples

Those of US who identify as having an alternative lifestyle

(LBGTQ.)

Black Apples

"Supporting Our Survivors;" as a DAILY reminder

that untreated addiction is both progressive and fatal.

by debra harman miller

Bruised Apples Mentoring Program members celebrate World Mental Health Awareness Day 2021 at Austin Galano Club, (standing L to R) with Thomas Terbay, Dave S., Jenny H., Deb B., 2021 Bruised Apples Group Facilitator and Peer Support Specialist Tom Cook, and Marc Hancock. BAMP Founder, Don Ellerbe (kneeling) in front with Diamond Deb and Ruby Tuesday.

by debra harman miller

We are the Shac

Change our
words,
change our
world!

Help Eliminate...

Mental

Health

Stigma

Derogatory comments connecting the symptoms of a severe mental illness to ordinary people places and things. In the statement "This weather is so Bipolar," for example, a more inclusive and accurate word choice might have been, "unpredictable."

Part III

Members of AAMHC share their experiences as they navigate their recovery journey providing

LIVING PROOF

that a mental health diagnosis is not the end of the world, but an opportunity to live life more fully.

by debra harman miller

We are the Shac

by debra harman miller

Bear   *2019*

One of the greater mysteries at the SHAC was Ole Bear's real name. However, wanting to share how much Austin Area Mental Health Consumers has blessed his life led *John Shurley* (aka Bear) to disclose that and much more about himself.

After moving to Austin over a decade ago, he has experienced chronic homelessness. Bear shares he prefers camping in the nearby woods to the bleak conditions he has experienced within shelters. Emergency shelters were designed for persons who were temporarily displaced and overwhelmed by loss, which *definitely was not* Bear's situation. He shares he appreciates the support from others at the SHAC in dealing with his severe depression.

--- --- ---

Bear is an artist, and for over a decade, he has crafted leather-work projects and created jewelry to get by. He carries a prototype of his ornate black leather backpack and scavengers for supplies for the handmade jewelry he crafts from strips of leather, crystals, gemstones, and pieces of the broken jewelry he collects.

by debra harman miller   41

We are the Shac

The separation from society is often more difficult to face than the scarcity of resources. While many lead a life of deception and are ashamed of their circumstances, Bear offers that the most pressing challenges he faces are finding a hot shower and having a place to store his belongings during the day when he is away from his campsite.

In 2019, Bear shared about a change in his way of thinking. As he was walking in the mornings in the woods, he kept finding two twigs on the ground, one laying on top of the other. At first, he shared, he blamed other campers and thought the "crosses" he found on the ground were some sort of practical joke. However, he soon arrived at the understanding that it was a personal message to him, *a call to action.*

Bear shared how he had recently been spared from a serious health challenge. He confessed he had quit drinking and had curtailed his time on the internet. With his newfound purpose in life, he began reaching out to others, and sharing his testimony.

He accepted being homeless as his lot in life and made the best of it by coming by for the noon *SHAC Snack* of a delicious soup or joining the *Bruised Apples* group on Mondays for tacos.

by debra harman miller

The supposition that the homeless are lazy, dirty, and desperate creates stigma which Bear oft-times finds more difficult to face than the lifestyle itself.

by debra harman miller

Bear *2020*

Although he made the decision to move indoors after his epiphany, most of the waitlists were closed. Often there is a year-long backlog of applicants waiting for the opportunity to apply and to qualify for them. Whenever low-income housing does become available, applicants must gather documents and respond quickly to accept the offer.

The homeless are often eliminated from the waitlist without warning. Bear had made almost daily use of the new computer lab at the SHAC prior to COVID-19. Although it was difficult to keep a cell phone or even the same phone number, access to the computer lab provided the connection he needed to complete the process.

For Bear and many others,

the Self-Help & Advocacy Center

was the key that opened the door

to their new home.

by debra harman miller

Christine
Mendez
2020

by debra harman miller

We are the Shac

Christine Mendez 2020

Christine joined the SHAC at the suggestion of her caseworker in 2018. Her caseworker believed the opportunities to take part in the peer support groups would aid her in managing her co-occurring health problems. When she learned more about Austin Area Mental Health Consumers services, she began one-to-one peer mentor sessions with her Mental Health Peer Specialist, Donald Seamster.

Christine attends the *General Support* discussion group as well as the Tuesday *WRAP©* class. She hoped she could learn to be more self-reliant but found sharing about her issues with others in the discussion groups also tremendously empowering.

One-to-one sessions can be very emotional; however, in the long run; she finds them very beneficial. She appreciates the opportunity to discuss her issues. Afterward, "my luggage didn't seem so heavy." The support groups have helped her with personal relationships and coping skills.

Besides mental health challenges, Christine shares she has also struggled with trauma. Recovery from Substance Abuse was also not new to Christine. She shared she had once "been sober" for over seventeen years but had since relapsed. In her sessions with her peer specialist, she sets goals for herself, including continuing along the path of her recovery journey.

by debra harman miller

Open your mind to see all people

Christine would like to thank the *Bruised Apples* group for their support! (See the Programs Part II section for more information on Bruised Apples Mentoring Program.)

At times, the SHAC is the only place she feels safe. "I had gotten more jittery and forgot how to be around people."

They accepted me for who I am. There were people just like me that really care!

One of her favorite groups is the *Healing through Beading* class wherein she made a trauma memory bracelet. Christine is interested in the *Job Readiness Program* and is eager to go back to college one day and continue her accounting degree. Christine shares she is looking into getting her own service dog in the future.

by debra harman miller   47

We are the Shac

Cynthia Patton *2017*

Cindi Patton grew up in an uncertain world as child who lived
with the extra challenges associated with Dissociative Identity
Disorder or *DID*. Early on, Cindi knew she had mental illness
because, "I had experiences I could not express to anyone." Her
first suicide attempt was at age 15. "I woke up and I did not
know where I was. It was scary." A strong faith carried Cindi
from institutionalized life to the independent, quirky, creative
woman she is today.

by debra harman miller

She shares coming to the SHAC has given her wellness tools that have allowed her to reduce the medications she takes that are often accompanied by physical damage over periods of extended use.

Because of this, she reports she feels much better today than she did before Austin Area Mental Health Consumers, Inc. at the SHAC became a part of her life in the 80s. During that period, there was less understanding about of what was then called *schizophrenia*.

Without patients having a say in their own treatment strategy, persons were treated primarily with strong sedatives which not only quieted the *"voices,"* but also took away the patients' ability to communicate their own needs. Previously, the medical model of treatment devalued and discredited patients' human rights but was believed to be the best practice at that time.

Few medical professionals had lived experience in either managing the symptoms or with taking the medications they prescribed to treat mental health disorders. Their lack of experience limited psychiatrists in their understanding of what medications worked on whom.

One doctor put it in these words: "Prescribing psychiatric medications in that era was like throwing spaghetti against a wall to see what stuck." He had no way of predicting which medication would work for which individual patient, or even

We are the Shac

why it was effective in some and not others. Although scientific advances led to the development of a new class of second-generation psychiatric medications approved by the American Medical Association in the late 80s, psychosis was still treated with Thorazine, Haldol, electric shock therapy, Lithium, and anti-seizure medications. Doses were increased until the patient or a family member reported the voices had quieted, which often masked the individual's emotional pain and disconnected the patients from themselves and others in order to quiet the voices that were problematic. Often patients "gave in" and reported the hallucinations had stopped to appease others, while they continued to face their symptoms in secrecy.

As a peer mentor in the early 80s, Cindi was aware of the connection to *Parkinsonism* and was relieved she could prevent others in her community from the side effects becoming permanent.

You could see it.... the dragged foot, the walk, no sense of smell. Physical disabilities, they call it, exacerbated by the anti-psychotics that function as a chemical straight jacket.

STRAIGHT JACKET ON YOUR MIND!

by debra harman miller

Open your mind to see all people

Cindi not only made her mark as one of the founders of the SHAC, but she also wrote about her experiences in a book that later was instrumental in writing the proposal for legislation that gave Texans with mental health challenges the right to access their own medical records.

Cindi continues, "I came back to the SHAC in a terrible crisis after taking benzodiazepines for 30 years. In 2016, Cindi tapered off the Klonopin with the supervision of her psychiatrist. Adamantly she emphasizes, *"I don't change my meds without my doctor."*

You have to trust your doctor!

The challenges of life with a dissociative disorder are far-reaching, especially in personal relationships. Cindi's long-term partner, Rick, is key to life outside an institution. "He's Golden, she sighs." At first, Rick "was freaking out" as her alters appeared; however, he grew to understand and respect her as a whole person.

Cindi copes by dealing with each thing as it arises in the now. As others living with Dissociative Identity Disorder or DID have discovered, Cindi says it best....

You Don't Have to Listen to the Voices!

We are the Shac

Revisions of the American Psychiatric Association Diagnostic and Statistical Manual (DSM) that classifies mental and physical disorders and conditions with codes that communicate the diagnosis between medical professionals and health insurance providers occur every few years.

Schizophrenia was replaced with a less stigmatizing label, Multiple Personality Disorder (or MPD.) Then, in 1984, the American Psychiatric Association voted to change MPD to a term that represented the spectrum of *Dissociative Identity Disorder* (DID.) Persons with the same diagnosis do not necessarily experience the same challenging symptoms or behaviors, and the concept of a spectrum reflects the person's unique combination of mental and physical symptoms that are chronic and disabling.

When questioned about her "alters" Cindi says she refuses to give them names, but describes them as *Angry, Demonic Me,* and *Forgetfulness.* Cindi warns "Everybody will eventually have a psychotic moment."

Cindi describes her experiences: "I have been **counselorized** by so many with labels." She shares her sense of hearing is exacerbated by disassociation. Sounds are often confusing, and she shares she often hyperspaces identities when she is under large amounts of stress.

As a member of the Board of Directors for the State of Texas Department of Mental Health Consumers, Cindi was one

by debra harman miller

Open your mind to see all people

of several of the original cofounders of what is now Austin Area Mental Health Consumers, Inc. at the Self-Help and Advocacy Center, (SHAC). As Cindi recalls, "It was NOT fun." She recants the first four years were the hardest thing she ever had to do, and that they prayed it would continue to keep on growing.

And Look at it NOW!

One quick, non-professional test for DID is to simply ask, "How many toothbrushes do you have?" Laughing, Cindi's response was "Of which kind.... *Six.*" She continues, *"It's hard to keep up with your identity."*

Thanks to her tools of mental wellness, Cindi's last suicide attempt was in 2000. Like many with mental illness, she had been couch-surfing for six months until "they just couldn't handle it anymore." Cindi found herself homeless and hopeless.

She has been very active in the SHAC; however, at times and like many others, Cindi has had to step back and focus on her own wellness. At the time of her baseline interview in 2017; she served as a contract resource director. At one time, she facilitated support groups as a part of Mental Health and Mental Retardation (MHMR) that was the county mental health authority in Travis County.

After a hiatus, Executive Director Ms. Shannon Carr encouraged Cindi to return. "Shannon is the best boss you could ever have." She prepared a desk for Cindi later in a more private

by debra harman miller   53

area when the stress of the high-profile job became counter-productive for Cindi's wellness. It was then that Cindi first set up her Wellness Recovery Action Plan, WRAP©, questions and solutions. She explains there is no need to discard and replace the plan as her recovery journey is fluid, and the key to recovery lies in letting her WRAP© grow with her.

Before the WRAP© class, there is a guided meditation which Cindi describes as "connecting to nature, a beautiful stream." During the group's meditation, members are directed to visualize a cool mountain stream and to place something on a leaf and watch it float away. Cindi remarks her first leaf carried away "everything that was bugging me.... I tried to put my boyfriend on the first leaf. *Later, I put myself on the leaf to see where everybody was going.*"

"I love to get a moment to sit down and talk with someone who just needs comfort that day." She explains everybody has to be a member to be here. Her experiences at the SHAC have taught her persistence. Cindi adds "don't give up if you find a place as magical as this. *Just don't give up!*"

As a member of Austin Area Mental Health Consumers, Inc., Cindi has held many distinct positions throughout the years. In 2017, Cindi submitted a proposal for a new group at the SHAC that brought a new support group to the members which encompassed knitting, macrame, crochet, and other handiwork. She named the group *Crochet with Cindi*.

Cindi Patton   2020

by debra harman miller

We are the Shac

Cindi spends less time at the SHAC now as she has a multitude of projects focusing on sharing her personal mental health recovery tools with others worldwide. One episode is *Cindi's Fish*, a mental health wellness tool she produced and launched on *YouTube*. Many around the world can now use Cindi's creation for mindfulness relaxation.

Cindi channels an enormous amount of her energy as she prepares the manuscript for her second book. At present, it comprises many of the short stories Cindi is crafting. She shares each is a snapshot of her lived experience. She uses another unique process that she begins by drawing a circle as a focal point with a constellation of details which resemble stars surrounding it.

Crochet with Cindi continues to be one of the most beloved groups because of the ways Cindi catered the class to fit the challenges of each individual member. The crochet class has a new facilitator, Donna Waggoner, and has been expanded and renamed *Hooked on Yarn*.

Cindi's adventurous spirit of trying new things and adapting them to serve the members' individual challenges is now, and always will be, the heart of the SHAC she helped found over four decades ago.

by debra harman miller

Cindi Patton
2021

Cindi Patton enjoys her COVID-19 Mental Health Wellness tool

MUSIC !

by debra harman miller   57

We are the Shac

Cindi has enjoyed the availability of the virtual *General Support Group* from her living room. She takes part regularly, something that would have been impossible through a recent medication change had she needed to come to the SHAC in person.

Bravely, Cindi posted on the SHAC's private Facebook page, Austin Area Mental Health ConsumersS, a video sharing her new wellness adventure, playing the electric guitar. She had always been interested in playing music and the COVID-19 quarantine was her stimulus to action. Cindi promises an update on her progress with her new Stratocaster, a gift from Rick, in the months ahead.

In December 2020, Rick proposed to Cindi, and she accepted. While they had planned to marry after the pandemic is resolved, *Cindi shares they are now setting the date for after they finish the remodeling on their new home!*

Congratulations and Best Wishes

Cindi & Rick

from all your friends at the SHAC!

by debra harman miller

Donald Ellerbe, LCDC *2017-2021*

Founder and Chair of the Board of Directors
Bruised Apples Mentoring Program, Inc., founded 2003

by debra harman miller   59

We are the Shac

Donald (Don E.) shares the grim fact that *thirteen* addicts die per hour in the US alone. However, the Center for Disease Control, the CDC, reports that number had increased 54 percent in 2020, which may be attributed to the isolation required to reduce the number of cases of COVID-19.

It was not incarceration, nor homelessness, nor a loss of family and friends, not even five inpatient stays at substance abuse treatment centers that could arrest Don E.'s addiction. Rather, it was opportunities for educational support from *AmeriCorps* that carried him from "sick, sad, and sorry," to freedom from active addiction. Don E. always adds *this time* when he refers to his clean date of April 18, 1997, to remind himself the journey of recovery requires vigilance.

Addicts in recovery can find

PASSION and

PURPOSE through

service to the community.

by debra harman miller

Open your Mind to see all People

A speaker at a conference in Waco, Texas in 1999, introduced Don E. to a peer mentor program for at-risk youth. In the presentation, she held up an apple and sliced it into sections to represent the teen participants who would scatter and plant new seeds of hope throughout the population. Inspired by her message, he raised his hand and asked if she thought her mentorship ideas for children could be applied to help alcoholics. Her response was devastating. Her failed marriage to an alcoholic motivated her to label all alcoholics as bad apples, for which there was *no hope of redemption.*

Don E. fumed all the way back home to Houston, Texas. Her "opinion" conflicted with everything he knew to be true. As he reflected upon his personal experiences attending the *Texas Unity Convention* held quarterly at The Lodge on Serenity Cove at Lake Whitney; he had already witnessed the **truth that the therapeutic value of one peer helping another creates an environment for recovery, that is without parallel.**

We Are the ShaC

Don E. steps ahead, leading the way to the Texas Unity Convention at the Lodge at Serenity Cove on Lake Whitney.

Bruised Apples Mentoring Program supports members as they attend this quarterly retreat for persons in recovery from substance use disorder.

Peer recovery was both documented and proven to be successful in twelve-step fellowships since the 1930s. The idea struck him....

by debra harman miller

We are *NOT*
BAD APPLES,
we're just a little Bruised.

From early in his recovery journey, *until* the Texas *Blizzardalooza* that hit Austin on Valentine's Day, in February of 2021, Don E. never detoured from the commitment he and many others make as they connect with nature and experience their first spiritual awakening at Serenity Point. For the past two decades, Don E. has attended every single one of the 80 Unity Conventions held quarterly.

In November of 2017, Don E. had been in intensive care following a heart attack when the Texas Unity Convention rolled around. He checked himself out of the hospital and loaded up supplies in the back of his pickup and set out to pick up his guests for the weekend. While others might think this action imprudent, they do not know how passionate Don E. is about recovery.

"Just don't quit NO MATTER WHAT" is the attitude of gratitude that carried him to work each day throughout the exhausting year of treatment for his Hepatitis C infection. Don E.'s energy and enthusiasm cannot be contained as he bounces into the meeting hall, wearing his trademark headgear; a green baseball cap with (two) three-foot-long chains of interlocked white key tags representing surrender.

The *Don E. experience* takes off as he guides the group and recants the symbolism of the twelve steps engraved in the stone beneath their feet. As he guides *Whitney virgins, (first time attendees,)* up the trail to Serenity Point, reverently, he encourages them to pick up a stone along the way. As they reach the twelfth step, an old wooden cross stands before them. Stepping gingerly, they creep to the edge of the cliff and hurl their rock *and perhaps a resentment* into the deep blue water below.

As he trained to be a licensed chemical dependency counselor over twenty years ago, he understood persons in early recovery not only need information and resources, but also *lots of hugs*. Because of this, Don E. opted to pause the *Bruised Apples* support group, until the City of Austin announced businesses such as AAMHC as the SHAC could reopen. Many treatment centers closed their doors during COVID-19, but Don E. adapted by learning new technology and now works for the State of Texas.

by debra harman miller

Don E. wishes to express his gratitude to Ms. Shannon Carr and the AAMHC Board of Directors for providing space for the *Bruised Apples Mentoring Program's* meetings over the past five years.

Deb B. and Don E. recharge their "spiritual batteries" at Serenity Point above Lake Whitney and stop to reflect upon the power of nature in recovery.

by debra harman miller

We are the ShaC

by debra harman miller

Donna Waggoner *2017*

Member of the Board of Directors
Austin Area Mental Health Consumers, Inc.

Donna has been a member of Austin Area Mental Health Consumers since 2010 and joined the board of directors five years later in 2015. She first heard about the SHAC from her neighbor, who was already a member. Donna says the biggest challenge she sees is how we can best serve the community and how we can make the SHAC more inviting. "Everyone is welcome," Donna adds.

Accepting the challenge of adapting existing groups from organic to virtual meetings over the phone or computer can be arduous for facilitators; however, Donna is excited she is able to continue the *Hooked On Yarn* group on Tuesdays. The "crochet" class includes many variations of handiwork including macrame, knitting, crochet, and embroidery. She shares that some members of the group even use sewing machines to do their embroidery because it is so much quicker.

Donna loves the *Meeting of the Minds* support group held the first Thursdays of the month, when attendance is larger because of persons paying for and picking up their bus passes. She feels the information brought into the SHAC from 2-1-1, Social Security and others has made a difference by letting members know about services that they may not be aware of.

We are the SHAC

When members develop questions about a needed service, the SHAC team researches the problem and invites persons from these outside organizations within our community to give presentations and to answer any questions the group may have about services offered in the Austin area.

Donna loves coming into the SHAC and "seeing everybody with a smile." She feels the ability of the leaders to keep everyone focused on the positive is "an awesome achievement." She shares when she first joined ten years ago, there were many people just hanging out. Now members are connected and involved in the programs. Persons coming in from next door at Integral Care are pleased to find out Austin Area Mental Health Consumers is a private entity and that there are things of interest to them.

As the City of Austin reopens, Donna is eager to meet in person so members can share what handiwork projects they have been creating during the pandemic!

by debra harman miller

Duff Brown *2017*

Duff came to the SHAC seeking information on how to use a computer. He was transitioning from a nearby sober living home to a more permanent home when a friend referred him to the computer lab. He was amazed to find volunteers at Austin Area Mental Health Consumers who offered to tutor him in the basics of the personal computer. Eager to make use of the services at AAMHC, he signed up for membership that day.

Duff said his expectation was that the SHAC was some kind of "Loser's Lounge," but was pleasantly surprised with what he found instead. With about four months sober, he had just gotten out of the hospital a couple of hours before with a broken nose, nursing a headache. For this reason, he asked that his photo be omitted from his story. Previously, he had signed up to volunteer his story for the book and was surprised to get

Then out of the blackness of my life

I thought

'Okay, I'll take the challenge!'

the phone call asking him to come in for the interview. He shared he rarely gets a phone call from anyone and "it was really a pleasant to wake up to a human voice over the phone."

He explained that his recovery program suggested he try new things that he did not want to do, such as reading books. *This time* he resolved to follow through and told himself that although he did not want to come, he showed up "because I know I need to do things I don't want to do in recovery." He added, that his first thoughts were about how he could get out of volunteering.

Duff shares he started smoking marijuana in 1968 to deal with the pressure he experienced due to a learning disability. Later when he moved to Austin at 19, he was introduced to harder drugs such as methamphetamines. "All the cops knew me from my drinking," he shared. One day an officer warned him, "Quit meth or we're going to arrest you!"

He also experimented with heroin for a while; however, that ended when he took the aluminum foil the black tar was wrapped in and scraped aluminum foil flakes into the mix. He remembers blacking out and waking up in St. David's Hospital emergency room where they were trying to save his life. He was ashamed, but the medical team convinced him it was especially important that he tell the truth. When he did, they could use a vacuum to suck out the aluminum. Two days later, Duff decided he had to quit everything and sought help.

Although Duff felt happy to be at the SHAC, he admitted he felt defeated. He expected he would "get deeper and deeper away from his success" if he lost his job and he was determined to study.

> *I listen now.*
>
> *I can't forget the horror,*
>
> *the suicide attempts,*
>
> *the depression,*
>
> *and the manic times.*

Duff was staying "just down the street" from the SHAC in transitional housing awaiting a move to sober living where he was looking forward to an environment with more supervision. The SHAC was the next right step, as he felt using the computer lab had empowered him to find resources and to make healthy choices in his recovery journey.

by debra harman miller 71

by d*e*bra *h*ar*m*an *m*iller

Harmony Dailey 2020
Certified Yoga Recovery Coach

Harmony (*aka* Tamara) drove past 3205 S. First Street for years and was intrigued at what the "Self-Help & Advocacy Center" sign meant exactly. A few years later in 2016, she made the decision to quit "drinking and doing drugs." She discovered a twelve-step group that is supportive of persons for whom the use of prescription medication is a necessary as a part of their recovery journey.

> *I have a diagnosis of*
>
> *Bipolar Disorder*
>
> *and ADHD and I was having a*
>
> *hard time fitting in when I attended*
>
> *other twelve-step meetings*
>
> *because there is a separate part of me*
>
> *that is not addressed.*

Harmony shares she soon joined a twelve-step group, and quickly found a temporary sponsor who had experience in facing the extra challenges she lives with.

After registering for the *Return-to-Work Program* with the Texas Workforce Commission Vocational Rehabilitation services in March 2020, the quarantine derailed her plans. When she read the *Job Readiness Program* at the SHAC included Mental Health Peer Specialist certification through *Via Hope,* she was eager to learn more.

It is not her symptoms that are problematic to Harmony as much as living with the **stigma** attached to mental health. She adds that although she may have a disabling condition; she does not have to be disabled from it.

In the past, when she disclosed her challenges to an employer or even persons who had known her for a while, she noticed a *"shift in perception in who I am... and what I am. It is as if I am no longer a whole person....* So, the advocacy program at the SHAC is awesome," she chuckles.

Like many others, Harmony loves the SHAC for the WRAP© program because her experience is that setting a routine and following it consistently improves her health.

Harmony was a panelist for the Bruised Apples Mentoring Program's 2018 *Toolkit for the Spirit Warrior* conference held during the month of May in celebration of Recovery

Month. The conference was created to raise awareness of potential physical damage from the over prescription of mental health drugs. Harmony presented information about her condition, *Hashimoto's,* wherein the thyroid is damaged. She attributes the damage to her thyroid to be the result of psychiatric medications.

In addition to traditional Western medicine, Harmony practices meditation, and employs the information she gained from a college nutrition course to search for ways to improve her health. During this time, she trained for a new career as a yoga recovery coach and has completed over 200 hours as a certified yoga recovery coach and another 300 hours in yoga therapy. She shares yoga provides her with a "huge mind/body/spirit connection."

My body was stuck in a fight or flight gear,

and yoga has given me the ability to find an

inner balance of

mind + body + spirit

without relying on addictive medications.

We are the ShaC

The WRAP©

takes some of that confusion (I live with) out of my mind. It gives me a clearer sense of direction.

by debra harman miller

She looks forward to certification as a Mental Health Peer Specialist that will afford her the opportunity to teach a seated yoga support group at the SHAC. She believes *"Pranayama"* is essential in regulating the parasympathetic nervous system. She shares that in the past, her nervous system was in overdrive.

One of the things she finds refreshing about her current psychiatrist, is that he has offered subtle suggestions (such as adding a multivitamin and omega three supplement to her treatment plan.) Her experience is that while additions such as these to a prescribed medication regiment are rare in a mental health setting, their addition has proven very therapeutic for her.

I have learned to advocate for

health care with a therapist and

I have a relationship with my doctor

Where WE work together!

---Harmony Dailey

by debra harman miller

We are the Shac

Helen loves Tai Chi

"It's just a slower form of Karate!"

by debra harman miller

Helen Mata   *2020*

A friend from church suggested Helen visit the SHAC for the *Half-Priced Bus Pass Program.* In addition, she was thrilled to find information about resources and a form of Martial Arts she could enjoy.

Transplanted to Austin from New York over a year ago, she had an early retirement from her career in pathology due to health problems. Her migraines were traced back to emotional trauma and "the stress of not ever talking about any of it." After the upcoming knee replacement surgeries, Helen's plan is to study medical billing and coding.

Helen is excited about the future and looks forward to bringing her two Siberian Huskies from New York home to her apartment in Austin.

by debra harman miller   79

We Are the Shac

Ivette Castro   2020
Mental Health Peer Specialist

When Ivette arrived at the SHAC for the *Half-Priced Bus Pass Program*, she already knew about *General Support* groups. She was pleased to find the new computer lab to work on her resume and cover letters for a job search.

As she looked around, Ivette envisioned ways she could be helpful to the underserved Hispanic community. In her lived experience, she feels Hispanics do not seek psychiatric help due to their cultural disposition of denying mental illnesses in general. Before COVID-19, she translated conversations during *General Support* groups, but it consumed a lot of the group time.

When AAMHC at the SHAC transitioned to virtual classes, Ivette created a Spanish-speaking *General Support* group. As a Mental Health Peer Specialist, she also does one-to-one peer mentoring and is fluent in both English and Spanish.

Three years prior, Ivette told people that she had shattered her right ankle in a *traumatic snowboarding accident* (that's her favorite story about the source of her injury.) However, the injury actually occurred when she was getting up out of bed. As a result of pain, she also suffers with depression. She did not receive a mental health diagnosis until November 2017. Ivette also manages her diabetic condition and works to create strategies for navigating her visual challenges.

by debra harman miller   81

We are the Shac

Ivette found creating her own WRAP© was helpful in making plans for self-care.

Occasionally a person may get a little rowdy because he or she is having a rough time, but Ivette is sensitive to the fluctuations inherent with mood disorders. At AAMHC at the SHAC, Mental Health Peer Specialists are always available to guide persons as they advocate for existing community resources. Peer-to-peer support provides a safe space to talk things over with someone who understands.

Ivette is enchanted by all things Disney and enjoys collecting souvenirs and Disney products. She confesses to seven trips to Disneyland in California, *so far*. However, she has traveled the 1,200 miles from Austin to Florida's Disney World *over 200 times*. Excited about the end of the pandemic in 2021, Ivette is eager to make her pilgrimage to the *Magic Kingdom*.

Monica Garcia assists Ivette

Castro as co-facilitator of the

General Support in Española

Each Thursday at 11:30!

by deBra harman miller

Jackie
Ruybal
2017

by debra harman miller

We are the Shac

Jackie Ruybal   *2017*

Jackie Ruybal, *"It rhymes with Bible."* Jackie is quick to point out as she signs the release form for the interview. A list of resources on the bulletin board at her senior living complex prompted her to ask around about AAMHC. She remembers a friend telling her "I'm not sure exactly what they do, but they help people." Although the information was vague, Jackie has an adventurous spirit and thought, "What do I have to lose?"

Isolation and a lack of transportation had left Jackie feeling a little useless; however, she was eager to try new things. So, she asked around some more and heard about the *Half-Priced Bus Pass Program* for Special Transit Services (STS or MetroAccess,) that is her only mode of transportation. As a "senior plus," life on a fixed income is challenging and "anywhere I can save money is a blessing to me."

> *I can't stand not being independent.*
>
> *I have to call, and I have to ask for help.*
>
> *It's not a door shutting in your face.*
>
> *You just have to catch it at the right time!*

by debra harman miller

Open your mind to see all people

Jackie enjoyed the *Meeting of the Minds* support group right away. The topic was Medicare and Medicaid insurance, which had been a source of confusion in the past.

She was impressed that the speaker took the time to answer every question and that by the end of the class, she felt that the gentleman had made things "crystal clear."

As she looked over the list of classes, she was extremely excited about the seated Tai Chi class scheduled for Fridays. She was eager to get more exercise but was intimidated by television commercials that show only young people going to the gym.

The computer lab and tutoring appealed to her as she was computer literate but was interested in the *Job Readiness Program.* She was excited to learn more about the *Volunteer Program* at the front desk as she was planning to update her computer skills.

Born and raised in Austin, *(Austinite,)* Jackie enjoyed working for the City of Austin and later the State of Texas Workforce Commission Vocational Rehabilitation services (TWC-VR.) They offered her a computer, and it was the first computer she had ever owned. Jackie thought, "I'm a real person now. I have a computer!" She was up for the challenge as she was stable because of her medications being adjusted. "So, it was easier to retain things."

by debra harman miller   85

We are the SHAC

Jackie was diagnosed with Bipolar Disorder and Post Traumatic Stress Disorder (PTSD,) and was unhappy with the concept of depending on the medications. She added she does not feel ashamed of her diagnosis since she had learned different ways of handling the PTSD which she feels is the result of violence from earlier in her life.

Jackie Ruybal   *2018*

Jackie made the decision that she wanted a better life and expressed an interest in twelve-step recovery. She was tired of drinking and said, "I want to die sober."

Once she made the decision to address her issues with recovery, Jackie made the commitment and connected with the *Bruised Apples* group, participating in the discussion group and other activities such as the Taco Fundraiser to purchase copies of literature for treatment centers.

As a volunteer, she answers the phones and does front desk duties such as checking persons in when they arrive. In the *Job Readiness Program* at the SHAC, members who are willing to commit to three days a week may apply.

by debra harman miller

Jackie
Ruybal
2018

by debra harman miller

We are the Shac

The opportunity for accountability rekindles a sense of integrity and members often report their stamina increases. Volunteers participate in a variety of ways from verifying resources for advocates to share with their peers, making coffee and serving drinks and snacks, to taking orders for the bus passes and distributing the passes on Bus Pass Thursdays three Thursdays a month. Once a month volunteers share ideas and concerns over a healthy lunch. They also have the opportunity to suggest creative ways to connect and support our peers.

> *I like to learn from my peers who have*
> *walked the walk,*
> *that have my diagnosis....*
> *I relate to them more.*

Executive Director Ms. Shannon Carr and Office Manager, Rita Barnes carefully screen members who apply and provide reasonable accommodations and supports for them to be successful in a variety of ways. Jackie enjoyed the working environment at the SHAC and began leading a much more active life. Her bright smile and new sober persona made her an asset as she greeted members and answered the phones.

by debra harman miller

Jody Bean   *2018*

by debra harman miller   89

We are the Shac

Jody came to the SHAC with Don E. after a meeting at Cherry Creek in 2018. He enjoyed the *Bruised Apples {{{SOS}}}* group but was dubious about other services.

Bruised Apples implemented a program of economic recovery for persons with dual diagnosis. The little-known Social Security program called the Plan to Achieve Self Sufficiency, (PASS,) protects the benefits of a person who depends upon government assistance. The business plan's objective may be self-employment or additional training for a new career.

Although the *Stop the Madness Media* program ended before Jody's paperwork could be completed, setting up his website and planning his company *MathWizard* was an exceptional learning experience.

Jody is active in social media. He shares from the heart the challenges and struggles he faces with isolation, recovery, and physical health issues.

Courageously, he is transparent with his fears and emotions, revealing his tenacity. Jody earned his BS in Pure Math from the University of Texas in Austin in 2004 and works primarily as a math tutor at Austin Community College.

by debra harman miller

The program to hire tutors is limited to parttime employment, which is not sufficient income for Jody to support himself. Although he seems quiet at first glance, he loves writing, board games, and *acting*. Jody also volunteered on the Board of Directors as Treasurer for Bruised Apples Mentoring Program in 2019.

Jody Bean

2021

by debra harman miller

We Are the SHAC

John

"welcome to the SHAC!"

Riley

Volunteer

by debra harman miller

John "*Welcome to the SHAC*" *Riley*   *2020*

Volunteer Program

John's sparkling voice greets each person as they enter the SHAC building. Early on, he realized the importance of seeing a familiar face. He remembers clearly how another volunteer, Rebecca, told him about the *Half-Priced Bus Pass Program* for MetroAccess and invited him to come to the SHAC. The thing that really impressed him most was that when he made it to the SHAC to learn more about the bus pass program, Rebecca herself greeted him.

He had his first experience in Self-Help and Advocacy that same day when he realized he had left his cell phone on the bus. Rebecca helped him contact MetroAccess, who retrieved and delivered his phone. Like many others, John was moved to want to give back to the SHAC and to be of service. He applied for the position as a volunteer and interviewed with the office manager.

John attends most of the classes at the SHAC, but it was in the *Tai Chi with Thomas* class that he developed a sense of belonging... a sense of family. John shared that when he first met Tai Chi Thomas, he literally offered to share the spare change of clothes he carries with him if the need should ever arise. Experiencing the ways Thomas met the challenge of being away from home for such a long period of time inspired John to think of ways he too could help others through peer mentorship.

by debra harman miller   93

We are the Shac

John participated in a ministry in Houston, Texas before coming to Austin. He enjoys an occasional excursion on *Megabus* to visit family and friends.

After he completed his WRAP© I certification, his next goal is to become certified to facilitate his favorite class, WRAP©. John is passionate about serving as a Mental Health Peer Specialist in the future.

John joined the *Volunteer Program* long before the pandemic began in 2019 and has continued as a Volunteer responsible for making *"warm calls"* to connect members with information on resources within our community, and to provide other supports. One such program included the delivery of boxes of food that were donated by Capital Area Food Bank and were delivered by MetroAccess drivers to MetroAccess clients' residences upon request.

Members shared that they were struggling to obtain resources due to the quarantine and were in "lock-down" for personal health reasons for over a year. The information on resources as well as the feeling of continued connection during the isolation proved beneficial as members reported the calls were a welcomed break.

John enjoys learning new skills and is especially pleased at the prospect of one-to-one tutoring sessions in the computer lab. Eager to help others, John has learned that when he sits and

by debra harman miller

listens to someone, he is often surprised to hear something different from what he expected to hear.

Personally, John has found the peer support he receives at the SHAC beneficial as it helped him to overcome some things, he felt were previously embedded within him.

The COVID-19 pandemic was especially hard on John and other members who did not have smart phones. Without internet service, some had cell phone plans with limited minutes each month. Persistent members such as John called in by phone and could take part in the discussions; however, they could neither see nor be seen by others in the group. All the digits that had to be dialed to join the *Zoom* groups took much patience and tenacity. Despite not being able to see people's faces in the groups that were talking since he dialed in by telephone, John enjoys the games on *Wednesday FUN Day,* exercising in the *Tai Chi with Thomas* group, and sharing in the *General Support* group discussions.

Eager for the reopening, John looks forward to the hybrid meetings that accommodate those who have not yet been vaccinated and those who do not yet feel comfortable emerging from the quarantine.

We are the Shac

LaTanya
Titus
2016

In memory of

LaTanya Titus

and many others who have passed through the SHAC.

LaTanya Titus   June 29, 1975 – December 28, 2017

by debra harman miller

Don't pin your insecurities on ME!

LaTanya came to the SHAC in 2013, looking for the half-priced Capital MetroAccess bus pass; but she found so much more. "We get to talk about real issues in our life in a variety of ways."

She is fond of all the *General Support Groups* on Thursdays and Fridays, but the WRAP© group on Tuesdays is her very favorite. She especially likes the groups because they are small and personal. "Don always supplies a wonderful meditation." In addition, she shares that she loves the variety of speakers who come to the SHAC for the *Meeting of the Minds* support group.

Quick with her contagious smile, LaTanya welcomes new and old friends alike. With empathy and compassion, she disarms the fear of being in a new place for many with her cheery disposition. Clearly, she genuinely cares about her "SHAC family." The physical challenge she lives with do not define her.

by debra harman miller   97

You don't have to be afraid

look at us!

We aren't contagious.

WE

are real people

And we are not going

away because

YOU are afraid

of what you do not understand.

by debra harman miller

I learned to say

*I **live with** Cerebral Palsy...*

*NOT **I Am** Cerebral Palsy.*

LaTanya shares openly about the events that caused her disability: "I have what is called cerebral palsy. It occurs either at birth or right after birth. It occurred during my birth. The umbilical cord got wrapped around my neck and it cut off my oxygen for a long time and I ended up with Cerebral Palsy."

After graduating from high school, LaTanya attended college, majoring in English. She aspires to return and finish her degree one day. She attributes her time at the SHAC to re-discovering her self-confidence and ambition.

LaTanya does not feel *DIS*-abled by her physical limitations. "I am an actual person who lives with a condition." Learning about self-care; that her feelings were validated; and that she has many options are just some of gifts of being a member of the SHAC that LaTanya cherishes.

We Are the Shac

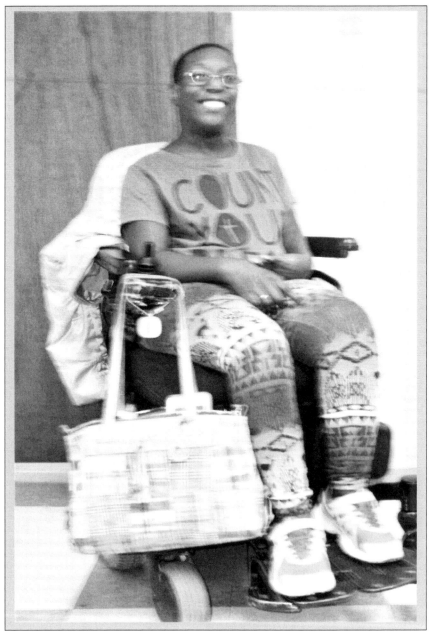

*by de*bra *har*man *mi*ller

LaTanya Titus   2017

Although the SHAC enriches her life, LaTanya is hardly isolated. She is a very active member of St. John's College Heights Baptist Church, and MetroAccess bus drivers look forward to driving her in her pink motorized wheelchair to church every week. LaTanya stays active at the gym with physical therapy and even goes bowling in her pink power scooter. She feels the SHAC has helped her become a better citizen, eliminated her stage fright, and improved her character.

> *I have a right to say 'NO,'*
>
> *and it is okay to be....*
>
> # *Just to BE.*

LaTanya shares "I am much happier and the SHAC is part of the reason because of the tools I learned here. I think it is an awesome place. It is a safe place to come, especially when I am frustrated. It's a very safe environment."

by debra harman miller   101

We are the Shac

by debra harman miller

Mary Ellen Sanchez   *2017*

Mary Ellen joined the *Crochet with Cindi* group wherein she appreciates the freedom to choose which project to tackle next. She is excited to share with others in the group and enjoys the support she receives from her peers as a part of the crochet class.

The anxiety Mary Ellen lives with (besides blindness) can be overwhelming. However, as she kept coming to the SHAC two days a week, she shares, *"things just got better."* As she continues to work her WRAP©, she gains new wellness tools to manage her symptoms.

Mary Ellen shares she feels a sense of belonging with her SHAC family. "They love and support me." She believes the diversity of the SHAC has taught her to respect all people. The spirit of inclusion has taught her to be more understanding of others. She is more active in her community now. Not only does she feel she has become better at communication; she believes what she has to say has merit.

By attending the *Meeting of the Minds* group, Mary Ellen gained a better understanding of the health insurance options available to persons who depend upon Social Security Disability Insurance (SSDI) benefits. She shares she looks forward to hearing the guest speakers each month. She appreciates the way this group is geared toward inviting speakers who are know-ledgeable and can address their concerns.

We are the ShaC

Some of Mary Ellen's activities outside of the SHAC include her Wednesday night ladies *Bible* study that helps her expand her circle of friends in the community.

Like many at the SHAC, Cindi Patton and Mary Ellen's friendship extends beyond their time at the SHAC. At their closing interviews for this book, in 2020, the two continue to meet at Cindi's home one day each week. The pair enjoy lunch and share their love of crochet and playing music.

At home, she uses her cell phone to play soothing music to provide the relaxing atmosphere she experiences at the SHAC that she feels is helping her improve mentally. She also enjoys movies, reading books in Braille, and helping others in their wellness journey. To Mary Ellen and many others, the SHAC is the most important place in the world!

Cindi Patton and Mary Ellen Sanchez

Mary Ellen shares this beautiful, crocheted blanket she created during the Pandemic.

by debra harman miller

Michael Sumuel   2017

by debra harman miller

Michael Sumuel   *2017*

Like many, Michael's mental health journey began with an accidental overdose rather than an unsuccessful suicide attempt. In the ensuing three months of hospitalized treatment and in attending aftercare, Michael established a new way of life that did not include running away from his past. This was not his first period of abstinence. His previous attempts were unsuccessful as marital discord and later divorce took its toll.

Inpatient treatment provides a safe environment to examine the past, including childhood traumas. As he faced and began healing from the events that led him to active addiction that began as a youth, he took responsibility for his past decisions and connected with others. In doing so, his desire to make a difference for others with a history of incarceration; particularly repeat offenders like himself, was his priority. He believes not only in second and third chances; but embodies the truth that most persons do not get and stay sober on their first attempt despite the consequences of returning to active addiction. Michael intrinsically chose a new future as a licensed chemical dependency counselor and *took action!*

Michael's first visit to the SHAC was to meet a classroom assignment for his Austin Community College degree plan. He experienced a one-to-one peer session with Mental Health Peer Specialist Donald Seamster. He reports he felt an instant rapport with him, and the connection and identification allowed him to share openly about his challenges. The hour of peer support reassured Michael that he, too, could make a difference in the lives of others.

After the one-to-one peer mentor session, Michael was invited to join in the *{{{SOS}}} Source of Support* meetings of *Bruised Apples Mentoring Program, Inc.,* and was pleased to meet *the other Donald* (Don E.) Ellerbe, LCDC who has facilitated the co-occurring disorders group at AAMHC since 2017.

The two had been incarcerated during the same years, but in different prisons. Both had been in and out of trouble since their youth and heredity was a major factor in both of their addictive patterns. Don E. shared how his passion for helping others beat recidivism, changed him, and gave him purpose and a sense of family.

As Michael was nearing the end of the formal classroom training at Austin Community College, it was time to begin his internship. He was concerned about where he could fulfill his supervised internship that did not include working inside the prisons he had fought so desperately to graduate from.

Don E.'s lived experience that a prior felon could find work in private and government facilities was uplifting to Michael. Soon afterward, his college advisor at Austin Community College connected him with a private treatment center to fulfill the supervised hours required to become a Licensed Chemical Dependency Counselor.

We are the Shac

Michael shared an older sister encouraged him to further his education. It had been over two decades since his last formal education was interrupted by the disease of addiction.

He shares that his sister's support and belief that he was capable of success helped him to turn his life around. Efforts by his mother and others had been unsuccessful in the past and he felt embarrassed and was defeated by past failures. He shares **his mother never gave up on him** throughout his addiction.

by debra harman miller

Open your mind to see all people

She had done everything in her power to prevent the family's genetic pre-disposition from ruining the bright future she envisioned for him. Like many parents, she tried to control his consumption by monitoring it at home. However, Michael's desire to fit in with his schoolmates was interrupted as he quit sports and did "research" on substance abuse.

He shares his mother never gave up on him throughout his addiction.

The boredom of prison life often leads to fantasizing about freedom and what the person's intentions are upon release. Most talk about the liquor store, the drug dealers, or sexual relations as their first pursuit. *This time,* Michael understood the dangers of that entitled attitude. Upon release, he shares he did not get off the bus for even a pack of cigarettes as he headed straight home to family. On the way, he prayed and surrendered to God's plan for his life. Many describe this as the *Spiritual Experience sufficient to bring about recovery.* Michael is not shy about his relationship with his Lord, and personal savior, Jesus Christ; however, he realizes the workplace is not an appropriate setting for witnessing. He hopes that others will see the changes in him and inquire about his personal journey, giving him an opportunity to share his path to faith when asked.

We Are the Shac

by debra harman miller

Michael Sumuel   *2020-2021*

Michael is also disabled by severe back pain from an earlier injury. To allow him to attend school and work in a treatment center, he had a nerve stimulator implanted in his spine. The electrical current in the stimulator interrupts the pain signal from reaching his brain but does not treat the spinal problem itself. The implant allows him to pass on opiates and to operate a motor vehicle safely.

Despite the financial challenges of living on social security and attending school, Michael has held onto his spotless blue pickup truck by taking his hobby of garage sales and reselling the items later to a new level. He also is of service in his community as others ask him to "keep an eye out" for the items they need for their new lives. Whether they be a disabled neighbor or a person in recovery, Michael is known for his abilities and willingness to help others with medical equipment such as a rollator for a new neighbor in crisis. He routinely searches through the unwanted and discarded items, and "upon request" helps others furnish their apartments as they begin their new lives in recovery whether it be physical, mental, or spiritual.

Michael shares he has never lost sight of his sobriety and his willingness to help others. At the time of the closing interview, Michael eagerly awaits an end to the shutdown, he explains that he is just a *hands-on person.*

by debra harman miller   111

We are the Shac

Meeting virtually makes it hard for both the counselors and the parolees and probationers. Michael shares the principal thing for him during the COVID-19 shutdown is a relaxation period after three strenuous years of college.

The mindset of having a chronic disabling condition can, at times, be aggravating, Because of this, he feels accepting a full-time position would not be beneficial to him due to the surmounting medical expenses and continual need for medical interventions to allow him to lead a full life. Like so many, his plans must be on hold at present as he is included in one of the high-risk groups awaiting the vaccine.

It (graduation) was a goal

I accomplished,

and I walk proudly everyday

knowing I accomplished that.

by debra harman miller

Ms. Rita Barnes   *2017*

Staff Administrator

by debra harman miller   113

Ms. Rita Barnes   *2017*

Staff Administrator

Rita was enroute to the YMCA when a MetroAccess driver told her about the SHAC's *Half-Priced Bus Pass Program*. She started out as a member, then became a volunteer, and just earned a position as Staff Administrator. Rita wears a plethora of hats as administrator: data entry person, receptionist, class facilitator, and go-for.

As a facilitator herself since 2014, Rita enjoys research-ing additional information for her groups to make them fun and interesting. Because of this, Rita finds she reads a lot more than she used to. She strongly believes one should **never stop learning.**

Before coming to the SHAC, Rita had always felt inferior because of a traumatic childhood illness. Much like the pan-demic now, prior to finding a vaccine for the poliovirus in 1955, there was a forty-year period wherein paranoia across the United States required extreme measures.

Rita was born in 1954 and contracted spinal meningitis and the poliovirus and was quarantined in Brackenridge Hospital from eighteen months until she woke up one day at two years old. She recalls her first memory is of a mermaid painted on a sea-foam colored wall in front of her as she pulled on the metal bed railing and stood up.

by debra harman miller

Open your mind to see all people

During the time they hospitalized her, two dramatic events changed her life. First, the need to contain the fatal disease kept infant Rita separated from all the other babies in the nursery. When whooping cough broke out in the nursery, she was the only baby to survive because she had been separated from the others.

The second consequence was nerve damage from the spinal infection, which resulted "mangled fingers and mangled toes" when she was left lying on her left arm too long and it cut off the blood circulation. All her life, Rita has beaten the challenge of having only one functioning arm. She learned to tie her shoes and button the buttons on her dresses using only one hand. She has had many surgeries throughout her life, but still cannot wiggle her fingers or toes. Rita has spent six decades in physical therapy of one type or another and holds multiple gym memberships. To the outside world, Rita's walk may seem slow and awkward. However, the training, skills, and balance required for her to stand and walk across the room are no less strenuous than any ballerina.

As a child, Rita felt inferior because the spinal damage left her with a limp and uncontrolled muscle spasms. In the early 1960s, bullying was common. Her teachers joined in and even encouraged her classmates as they encircled her, spitting and casting insults and pennies. Rita's response was "It was just money, so I picked it up." By the time high school rolled around, she had gathered 600,000 pennies. (Rita saved the entire

$6,000 for over a decade, then selected her first automobile in the 1980s.)

"I was always wrong; I was always the problem" was the *lie* she accepted. Volunteering her time at the SHAC built her self-confidence. She says she was good at being a loner; but prefers to be with people now.

One-to-one peer support has given Rita a fresh perspective and has opened her mind to other possibilities. As part of the *Job Readiness Program*, AAMHC has supported Rita with opportunities for training through *Via Hope* as a Mental Health Peer Specialist and with computer and management skills through Austin Community College. The job readiness skills are an important part of the consumer-run nonprofit. Rita came to the SHAC with some self-taught skills: Spanish, basic computer skills, and American Sign Language. Not only does Rita have an associate degree in General Studies from Austin Community College; she was among the 60-70 people who founded ACC.

by debra harman miller

Open your mind to see all people

Ms. Rita Barnes *2018* *Office Manager*

by debra harman miller 117

Ms. Rita Barnes   *2018*

Office Manager

A year later, Rita shared the history of the support groups at the SHAC. At its inception, the groups were all discussion groups and were named according to the current diagnostic labels, such as the bipolar support group and the schizoaffective disorder group. As she facilitated these support groups, Rita responded to the concerns from group members.

They expressed the way the groups were named after mood disorders made them feel like they, too, were merely labels. So, with the help of the membership, new group names were chosen. The group expressed a need just to talk about things in general, so the name changed to the *General Support* group that meets each weekday.

In January 2018, Rita received a scholarship from the SHAC and was preparing to attend training with *Via Hope* the next month (February 2018) at the time of her second interview. Rita was promoted as Office Manager at the SHAC and was seeing even more possibilities for herself in the near future.

As the Office Manager, Rita had embraced the challenge of recruiting members for the Volunteer Program to staff office positions. She finds while she might predict volunteers' capabilities; they often surprise her as they deliver tenfold.

by debra harman miller

Conversely, she often finds it helpful to reassign tasks to allow a person to take part, even though "maybe it's not their day."

While 2017 was filled with opportunities, Rita still limited her world with negative self-talk such as 'I can't, I shouldn't... I won't!' As she developed management skills, she has found an inner voice that shouts, "I can, I will... and where do you want me?" This attitude has given her the courage to speak not only as a group facilitator but also to speak at local hospitals and within the community to share about the programs offered at the SHAC.

Look at this place...

It's like an empty shell

and we get so much

out of it.

We are the Shac

by debra harman miller

Ms. Rita Barnes   *2019*

Office Manager – Mental Health Peer Specialist

Technology problems plagued the volunteer staff when a new telephone system was installed to better track the services the SHAC provides as the membership grew to over 1,300 in 2019. Keeping track of members' calls for help to find resources such as food was of paramount importance to both Rita and *also* to the person asking for help. The challenges of re-training the volunteer office staff were arduous, but Rita was persistent.

Rita shares her most rewarding accomplishment over the past year was to affect change by working with the City of Austin officials to make the SHAC building more accessible. She was concerned about the members' safety as they arrived at the SHAC in wheelchairs, walkers, and other assistive devices. Because of the scramble to complete the required classes and pick up the reduced fare bus pass on Thursdays, it was unsafe to load and unload the many physically disabled members. Her persistence paid off as the city officials re-zoned 84 feet (enough space for four busses) a bus-only lane.

Karena points out the new bus-ONLY parking zone!

We are the ShaC

Ms. Rita Barnes *2021*

Office Manager   *Mental Health Peer Specialist*

Ms. Rita not only met her goal, earning Mental Health Peer Specialist Certification, she completed ACC classes in a variety of computer programs such as graphic design and attended workshops where she earned many Continuing Education credits or (CEU's.)

by debra harman miller

Open your mind to see all people

When the SHAC closed its doors to the members on March 15, 2020, there was a new scramble. Often, new members arrive without stable housing. As the Executive Director, Ms. Shannon Carr, and her assistant reconciled the membership roster with the new member's forms, they discovered many contacts were obsolete or missing vital information.

Although the classes were already inclusive of visually challenged persons, new strategies for adapting the groups for interactive participation were created. This customization proved crucial in transforming the organic support groups into virtual groups over the *Zoom* platform when the need arose.

Finding ways of supporting the membership while the City of Austin is closed for business to contain the spread of COVID-19 put to task more training within the office staff. Some volunteers were no longer available, while others were eager to get more involved. Volunteers needed additional forms created to document the services provided during the shutdown and to allow more volunteers to help from home while making "warm calls" to check on members.

At the age most persons retire, Rita starts her bachelors' program this year. She continues her vigorous exercise program and enjoys meeting with friends for lunch. Occasionally she leaves her leg brace at home to step out in a pair of stylish boots.

by debra harman miller   123

We Are the Shac

by debra harman miller

Ron Hillard   *2020*

Ron migrated to Austin from Louisiana in the wake of the hurricane Katrina disaster. Complications from an automobile accident diminished his vision and drew him to Austin's Criss Cole Center, (that stands across the street from the Texas School for the Blind and Visually Impaired.) After completing the training in just three months, Ron followed the suggestions of his caseworkers from the Texas Workforce Commission Vocational Rehabilitation program and from the Department of Aging and Disability guiding him to AAMHC at the SHAC for the *Half-Priced Bus Pass Program*. Ron signed up with the SHAC that day and stayed over for his first peer support group to begin.

Utilizing MetroAccess services, Ron works parttime at a local pizzeria constructing cardboard containers. He lives alone but enjoys getting out and being active. It is his love of the people at the SHAC that makes him feel at home. "There's just a different environment. You can feel it when you walk in the door. It's a good vibe." Ron shares he treasures AAMHC at the SHAC because it motivates him to "get more learning in, and to have somewhere to go for at least a couple of hours of the day."

His favorite classes are the *General Support* group and the *Meeting of the Minds* group on Thursdays. Going to the SHAC and attending the support groups allows him "to get to talk to everybody." He reports he especially appreciates the

We are the Shac

information shared about resources in the Austin community in the *Meeting of the Minds* support group. Ron also loves the *SHAC Snack* program and especially enjoys the soups the Hospitality Leader, Virginia Leybas, prepares. Quick with a smile, Ron likens himself to the *Cookie Monster*© as he loves to tease the others about snatching up their share of the loot from the many desserts and snacks available to take home each day thanks to generous donations to Austin Area Mental Health Consumers, Inc. at the SHAC from local businesses such as Randall's, HEB, Central Market, Whole Foods, as well as individuals within the Austin community.

Ron studied JAWS, (a computer program created for visually impaired users,) as part of his training at the Criss Cole Center, and he looks forward to one-to-one tutoring sessions in the computer lab as the SHAC reopens. In the meantime, Ron has joined in the *General Support* group. At first, he found it overwhelming to call into the *Zoom* directory to take part in the ongoing virtual support groups each day. He advocated for himself and asked another member to help him find an easier way to access the classes through the internet instead of dialing the meeting number and pass codes by telephone. Using the calendar feature Google provides in his cell phone, and an email sharing the link that now pops up on his phone in a timely manner; with one click, he launches the *Zoom* platform to join the *General Support* group.

by debra harman miller

Ru' Kaiel Johnson

2020

Patient Advocate

AAMHC Board Member 2021

Ru' Kaiel discovered AAMHC at the SHAC while attending sessions at Integral Care next door. First and foremost, Ru' is a patient advocate, but caring too much has been a downfall for Ru' in the past. Overwhelmed, she had just given up on life until her son, who serves as her medical power of attorney, advocated

by debra harman miller

for her. Ru' experiences debilitating paranoia and often finds it difficult to go places. Since she found the SHAC, she says she enjoys being with friends and hanging out for the day. Disability is frustrating to Ru', who is legally blind. For a while, she had worked three jobs at a time. As stress built up, work was a way to stay focused and pretend like nothing was wrong. At other times, it is hard to get out of bed or to take a shower. "You just don't feel that bad," she told herself until her last hospitalization in 2018.

Coming to the SHAC, Ru' felt safe and could overcome her paranoia about using a computer. She did not trust the internet, and the SHAC was the only place she felt safe to watch *Netflix*. Since then, Ru' has her own computer area at home where she loves challenging herself with brain teasers and strategy games. However, her first love has always been reading, especially history.

Even if you are bedridden,

YOU

are still part of the community.

People value and appreciate your input.

by debra harman miller

Previously, Ru' worked in the Environmental Protection Agency and was certified as a safety regulations trainer to instruct the companies' training teams. In the future, Ru' would like to finish college in Information Technology and become a Head Librarian.

At the SHAC, Ru' tried both chair yoga and crochet for the first time. She was thrilled to find persons who had been doing them for a long while who were very patient. Ru' especially enjoyed the handouts about Tai Chi and loves going to the SHAC because she knows she can show up there intermittently and not be judged.

Ru' enjoys the *Bruised Apples {{{SOS}}}* group and finds her WRAP© very helpful. She also uses the calming room to meet with her caseworker. Working with a Mental Health Peer Specialist has helped disarm some of her triggers and has helped her cope with life while decreasing paranoid thinking. "In the past, it was hard not to feel weird if people haven't seen me for a while."

Ru' takes part in the Austin Film Society's training program to produce programs for Austin Public Access Television. They offer training on all major cameras, plus an editing studio. She has already worked as a producer for a project and is eager to create her own show on public television to share about...

ADVOCACY.

by debra harman miller   129

Steven Haag   2020

Steven found his way to the SHAC through a MetroAccess driver in 2018. His expectation was that he would find groups to talk about things and that the SHAC helped people. His passion is recovery and advocacy. Previously, he worked in collections after attending Wichita State University. A series of health emergencies (triple bypass, stroke, and memory loss,) compelled him to find his way with limited resources.

Instead of being bitter about his struggles, he shares his lived experience in navigating the healthcare, housing, and social services systems. Steven keeps detailed records of resources in a three-ring binder to share with others and is quick to offer his business card. While he performs volunteer work at Hope food pantry, his church, and attends twelve-step meetings, he is also being of service in another way.

He strives to be of service to his Higher Power as his path crosses with persons who are overwhelmed. Personally, he has found that just knowing about resources is only the surface. Steven finds his volunteer work has unknowingly provided him with a network of local government officials. They later advocated for him when he was hospitalized and could not make the deadline for filing a required housing renewal form.

Steven enjoys the *Meeting of the Minds* group and *Bruised Apples*. Despite his many health issues, he celebrates 26 years of sobriety in 2021.

One Blessed Day at a Time!

by debra harman miller

Thanks to Suzanne Edmiston Worrell for sharing this photo of a recent art show of her work. Suzanne was excited to share this special moment of accomplishment with her mother and biggest supporter, Patsy.

Suzanne Edmiston Worrell

Certified Peer Specialist   ***2020***

Suzanne was a member of a peer support group at the Recovery Center in 2007 when she discovered *Imagine Art,* (an Austin community of artists with disabilities.)

by debra harman miller   131

We are the Shac

Suzanne Edmiston Worrell

Certified Peer Specialist **2020**

She completed her Bachelors' degree in Studio Art at the University of Texas, followed by certification in Multi-media at Austin Community College. Suzanne had been afforded the opportunity to work with children with special needs in the Austin Independent School District as a substitute teacher, but her four hospitalizations for anxiety and dissociation from 1995 to 1998 complicated that plan.

As she took part in support groups, she became interested in a career as a Mental Health Peer Specialist. Using a twelve-step group for support, Suzanne lost 35 lbs. in 2006 and was interested in helping others. Suzanne loves to use art therapy as her personal wellness tool to help reduce the anxiety and the extreme paranoia that challenge her. She started by facilitating a few small groups at the Recovery Center which "bled over into the SHAC." As a Mental Health Peer Specialist, Susanne works as a contractor for AAMHC at the SHAC providing peer support groups for Austin Travis County Integral Care (ATCIC.) Initially, she led groups on art, health, and nutrition. When she joined the SHAC, Suzanne remembers feeling very supported by the other peer specialists, Cindi Patton, and Donald Seamster. Her nickname for him is the "Big Buda," and she finds his sense of humor uplifting. As a Mental Health Peer Specialist, she loves to carry the message recovery is possible for those with mental health issues. Seeing other

by debra harman miller

people flourish gives Suzanne lots of hope for herself. Until the City of Austin temporarily shut down businesses in response to the COVID-19 pandemic, Suzanne led groups outside the SHAC at Skyline Terrace, Almeda House, and the Right Step. However, through the *Zoom* platform, she is available to co-facilitate the HYBRID *General Support* discussion group.

For Mental Health Peer Specialists, training is ongoing. Recertification is every two years, and the MHPS requirement for continuing education is especially pertinent as peer support goes virtual. Besides the new technology, developing ways to connect which are interactive, inspiring, and personal must be explored by facilitators everywhere. Suzanne adds she finds sharing a reading is not as effective on *Zoom* as paraphrasing the information and directing those who are interested to the resource later. On the personal side, Suzanne finds sharing her story with others and talking with other people has made her more sensitive to others and the connection with others reduces her anxiety.

Some days, Suzanne is confident and engaged and others, "I have to just curl up in my bed and be in a fetal position." Suzanne combats these feelings by talking with others, journaling, practicing good nutrition, taking medications responsibly, playing with her dog, attending twelve-step meetings, walking, painting, and jogging. She enjoys lifting weights, using a personal trainer, and shares "exercise is good for the brain."

We are the Shac

by debra harman miller

Tana Kaldon *2017*

Tana found her way to the SHAC in 2004. She had heard about the peer mentorship services; however, it was two years later, following an unsuccessful suicide attempt, that she came in for help. When she checked with her doctor, she was told the soonest appointment available to her was two months away and she did not see how she could wait for an appointment from the therapists the hospital referred her to. When she came in for Peer Support, she asked for a person who was older and would understand the arduous task of being the caregiver for aging parents. She had been the caretaker of her parents and when it was time to face the tough decision to "pull the plug" for her mother's life support; it was more than she could bear.

Tana was matched up with Mental Health Peer Specialist, The Don Seamster, who also was a Veteran from the Vietnam era. She had little faith in the Veterans Administration services that were available to her because of the gaps in her father's care. Her peer specialist supported her by accompanying her to the VA to sign up for healthcare services which she says saved her life. Combining her veterans' services with the specialists and surgeons available through Medicare, she feels has made a tremendous difference in the quality of her physical and mental health wellness.

We are the SHAC

Undeterred by her challenges, Tana had no need for the discounted bus pass as she would raise and lower her own motorized wheelchair onto the back of her van and drive to and from her visits to the SHAC.

When asked what she would tell a friend about the SHAC, she replied that unlike many places, if you come into the SHAC in crisis, you will not be turned away or shuffled around for an appointment for another day. Although a person might need to wait a bit, she shares you can count on there always being someone to listen and provide support through advocacy.

During the pandemic, Tana was forced to quarantine, as she is plagued with many health problems, especially in her spine and hands. She finds great comfort in tending her garden.

Tana shares her favorite wellness tool is social media political discussions. She is eager to share about legislation, especially changes in policies related to mental health.

During the pandemic in 2021, she moved to a new home in the country. She shares she is very grateful that although she cannot physically come into the SHAC, she continues to receive the one-to-one peer services remotely. She would like to add that the quality of her healthcare has improved thanks to the individualized help she receives when she reaches out.

by debra harman miller

**THE DON -
Donald
Seamster**

*Certified Peer
Specialist*

2017

T*HE* DON –

Donald Seamster

Certified Peer Specialist **2017**

Members will be excited to learn more about The DON's history...

    The DON chose the military as a career after high school and proudly served our country for 20 years. During that time, he was stationed in Vietnam, Germany, and Panama. While he was stationed in New Jersey, he worked as a motion picture photographer. One of his accomplishments was in collaboration with the *New Jersey Shade Tree Commission*. They produced a film called *The Stripper* dealing with an invasive species of moths. This collaboration resulted in his military unit receiving an Academy award in the Documentaries category. He also received a Humanitarian Service award for his work with the *Jonestown Massacre*. He finished out his military career as a Master Instructor at Lowry Air Force Base in Denver, Colorado.

    After retirement from the military, he came to Austin and served ten years as a police officer at Austin Community College. While there, he achieved the rank of Sergeant. He attended

by debra harman miller

classes during his time at Austin Community College, earning an Associate degree in *Law Enforcement.*

After graduation, he continued his education by enrolling at St. Edward's University to complete his bachelor's degree in Human Services. When Don explored opportunities in Austin to do his internship, he contacted Executive Director, Ms. Shannon Carr to learn more about Austin Area Mental Health Consumers. As luck would have it, The Don chose the SHAC and when the internship ended, he was invited to become part of the staff as a Mental Health Peer Specialist.

With a keen sense of discernment and a sharp eye for detail, Don lends an ear as members share their challenges and experiences in recovery. He is sensitive to the struggles that each one of the members faces. As a Mental Health Peer Spe-cialist, he is unique in his ability to balance their crises with patience and empathy.

The Don opens the hour-long *General Suppor*t Group with his overwhelmingly popular guided meditation, *Leaves in the Stream.* With the soft oriental melody pouring from his laptop, The Don begins the guided virtual journey: a mindfulness exercise. As they attend groups, members report they feel their anxiety, pain, and fear disappear as his soothing voice guides the members through a field to a cool mountain stream.

We Are the Shac

by debra harman miller

THE DON –
Donald Seamster

Mental Health Peer Specialist Supervisor   **2021**

As the SHAC prepared to reopen in the summer of 2021, The Don celebrated his 71st birthday and continued his dedication to Austin Area Mental Health Consumers, Inc. by supervising new MHPS interns and Mental Health Peer Specialists. The Don was on the front line of the *"COVERT,"* (The Don's nickname for the sneaky pandemic,) as he was the first known case of the corona virus within the SHAC staff.

While many "seasoned Citizens" took their leave and retired when COVID-19 hit rather than adapt to the innovative technology required for classes on the *Zoom* virtual platform, The Don was resilient! When the *blizzardalooza* hit Austin hard on Valentine's Day 2021, despite the storm, while AAMHC was *(not at the SHAC,)* the team never failed to provide opportunities for peer support. The Don set up "headquarters" in a nearby hotel with functioning electricity and internet services. With the help of his team of Mental Health Peer Specialists, members could join in the virtual discussion groups using their cell data plan. Electrical providers were forced to "roll" electrical services and create outages on all nonessential buildings to conserve power strategically to keep the grid from shutting down entirely. The winter storm disrupted phone service and internet services and left many in the Austin area without heat and water for over a week.

SHAC members continued to attend the two support groups offered each day. Mental Health Peer Specialists provided one-to-one sessions by using their cell phone data plans.

As Mental Health Peer Specialist Supervisor, The Don has limited his participation as a group facilitator to focus on the *Job Readiness Program* at the SHAC. He supports new Mental Health Peer Specialists interns by sharing his lived experiences and shares that in addition, he also continues to grow in his own mental health recovery wellness journey.

Live so that when your children think of fairness and integrity, they think of you!

by debra harman miller

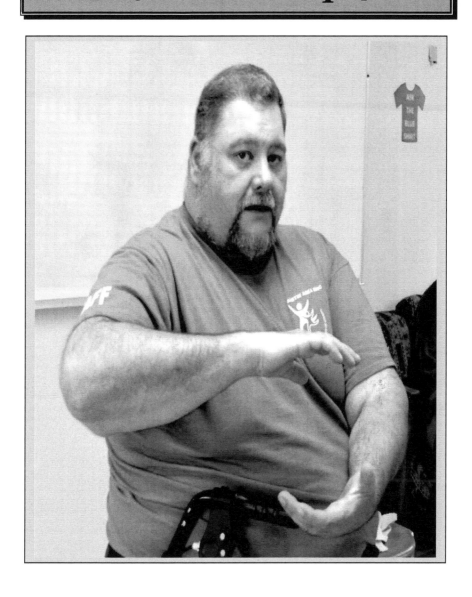

Thomas Terbay, Jr. *2017*

by debra harman miller   143

We are the SHAC

Inspired by the ways Rita Barnes faces her challenges, Thomas visited the SHAC three weeks later in the summer of 2015. He was not only interested in saving money, but also in saving himself from a deep depression. For ten years prior, Thomas isolated, and he remembers he was glad to be going somewhere besides his endless medical appointments.

Thomas grew up in Austin and was selected for a junior firefighter training program while attending Westlake High School. The enthusiasm of the young men soon led to greater opportunities and greater risks. Thomas wisely chose to attend nursing school after high school while he worked as an Emergency Medical Technician. He knew, like in sports, a career in firefighting was short lived. After completing the nursing program at Austin Community College, Thomas was awarded his nursing degree and he was off to fighting fires. He was hired immediately by a fire department in the Fort Worth area and loved the comradery with fellow firefighters as they drank and rough housed to forget about their days.

As Thomas grew more and more depressed, he was sent to a psychologist where they did an assessment and found his depression and anger (suicidal/homicidal thoughts,) to be "off the charts." Thomas' first inpatient treatment for his mood disorder occurred in 1990 and he was formerly diagnosed with bipolar disorder, rage disorder, PTSD, and extreme anxiety.

A month later, Thomas was released from the inpatient stay, eager to return to his life. Soon thereafter, Thomas was

by debra harman miller

scrambling down a ladder, hurrying to move to a better position to assist firemen on the other side of the blazing building when his boot slipped off the rung of the ladder. Barely 21, the fall ended his career ended almost before it began.

--- --- ---

The spinal damage from the landing was extensive; however, he shares his lowest point occurred sometime later when a viral infection manifested with temporary paralysis. He explains, often a limb is frozen with paralysis, yet at the same time, can be ablaze with searing nerve pain. The uncontrolled pain, the severe depression, the sudden loss of identity, (coupled with feelings of uselessness and relentless self-deprecation) imprisoned him. For Thomas, food was a welcome escape, and over time, his misery grew as he did. He reached an all-time low, weighing 645 lbs. when his mother passed away. After the infection was treated, the paralysis reversed, and Thomas woke up one day and decided to fight back. He began trudging the length of the Olympic sized swimming pool at the gym each day and soon joined the aquatic exercise classes they offered.

It was then he discovered Martial Arts (specifically Tai Chi and Qi Gong,) and over a three-year period, he completed the extensive program, earning his *Black Sash* at the martial arts school and was "kicking butt" teaching Tai Chi. The school, *Master Gohring's Tai Chi and Kung Fu,* was geared to older persons who wanted to try martial arts for the first time. The students did not consider themselves "athletes" by any means and the school training was designed to be adaptive to meet an array of challenges.

With persistence, Thomas burned off half of his body weight and was beginning to enjoy life again but was aware his health was deteriorating fast. In the past, every two years he found himself hospitalized for one medical crisis after another. Historically, he would spend four weeks in one type of medical facility or another and then head to an inpatient rehab immediately following.

When Thomas signed up for membership at the SHAC, in the summer of 2015, his interest was in peer support as well as the *Half-Priced Bus Pass Program*. He shares before he arrived, he expected to find the same cattle pen of long lines, disorganization, and the long wait he often experiences at his other medical appointments. He hoped to find insight on the problems he was carrying.

Since he lived with the label of "Bipolar Disorder," he was interested in what he could learn about himself in the bipolar support group discussions. Thomas was also pleased to find The Don (Seamster's) WRAP© support group. More than once, he has pulled out his hard copy of his WRAP© and has been able to see what was off with his mental and sometimes physical health and take action to stay healthy. He attributes a newfound ability to cope with living to the tools he is learning from his peers and from his one-to-one peer sessions. Thomas said he identified with his Mental Health Peer Specialist immediately and reflected upon how The Don Seamster's calm, soothing voice helped his anxiety.

After a year passed, Thomas felt the pressure to help in some way, but still struggled with feelings of inadequacy. Thomas knew he did not look like someone who was in good shape. Although he believed in his mastery of the martial art, he felt he lacked the confidence to speak in front of a group.

When he took a risk to volunteer to create the seated Tai Chi class, he felt alive for the first time in years. He prepared some handouts for the class to explain Tai Chi. His proposal was accepted by the Executive Director, and he began cofacilitating a yoga class which evolved into *Tai Chi with Thomas*. Normally tongue-tied in a group, Thomas found passion in sharing about the benefits of Tai Chi and adapting the class to fit the needs of the individuals who attend the Tai Chi class, just as he had done in his own training.

Thomas describes a sense of "family" from the friendly ways he was welcomed into the SHAC. The unconditional brotherly love he experiences there gives him a feeling of connection with other members. Thomas shares that it soon became apparent to him, "We all are a part of one giant organism; from the tiny, microscopic bug, to human beings." His experience of feeling interconnected at the SHAC frees him to venture out beyond the doors of the SHAC and *into action* as a part of the recovery community.

Thomas has other health conditions such as diabetes which often conflicts with his recovery from food addiction. Unlike other forms of addiction, total abstinence is not possible and daily maintenance is difficult to balance. Like many with mental illness, Thomas abused alcohol and other substances to relieve his symptoms. Coming to the SHAC is helpful for Thomas in managing his challenges because of the structure the groups provide. He reports after spending the day at the SHAC, he rarely feels the same compulsion to eat that used to control him.

The

Five

Hearts

Faith

Respect

Perseverance

Patience

Humility

by debra harman miller

Thomas Terbay, Jr.   *2018*

Assistant Admin.

Regeneration best describes the 20 months since that first interview. As Assistant Administrator, Thomas Terbay, Jr. continues to lead the Friday *Tai Chi with Thomas* class which is still

by *debra harman miller*   149

his favorite. Attendance has quadrupled. In addition, he occasionally facilitates his other favorite group, the WRAP©. Thomas finds it educational whether he leads the group or attends the Tuesday sessions as a member. On a deeper level, Thomas attributes his many achievements to employing the principles of the *Five Hearts* to everyday problems he used to ignore. Information and inspiration draw him to *General Support* group as well.

Thomas works closely with Administrator Rita Barnes, (the person who invited him to the SHAC.) Alternating days, Thomas and Rita provide leadership and match the tasks with the skill set of the office staff of volunteers. As a supervisor, Thomas is ultimately responsible for the accuracy and completion of data entry. One challenge is training volunteer staff members on a new phone system which still hits snags with multiple phone lines. Thomas has learned to deal with a multitude of crises as they arise.

At his baseline interview, Thomas shared he is just "not a goal-setter." However, a little under two years later, Thomas plans to expand his education in the future as he explores the mental health field. Becoming a Mental Health Peer Specialist is a goal he is considering. He jokes that being a paid employee at the SHAC "is both a parttime position and a full-time adventure!" Thomas commits to fourteen hours a week as a volunteer in addition to his administrative position. The influx of traffic in the small building can be overwhelming, especially on those hectic bus pass Thursdays when over a hundred of the members with varying mobility devices swarm the building to order and pick up their bus passes.

But that is only part of the story of Thomas' year. He found recovery and has earned his bronze18-month coin. In December 2018, he will be honored for achieving multiple years. He actively participates in four of the many twelve-step fellowships in the Austin recovery community, leading meetings and doing service work six days a week.

Between the SHAC, twelve-step meetings, managing his physical health challenges, counseling, working out at the YMCA, delivering the liturgy at his church, Thomas spends more time on MetroAccess busses than he does at home with his beloved dog *LuLu*. He estimates he takes over 88 excursions on MetroAccess each month. The trips to the SHAC are usually only 15 minutes but some other locations can consume as much as three hours' time. That *Half-Priced Bus Pass Program* monthly ticket saved Thomas over $3,000 in 2018.

Bruised Apples honors Thomas Terbay, Jr. with his 3-year "Certificate of Sobriety" in December of 2019.

Congratulations, Thomas!

We are the Shac

by debra harman miller

Thomas Terbay, Jr. *2020-2021*

Administrator

Mental Health Peer Specialist (Intern)

Thomas easily adapted his seated Tai Chi class to the *Zoom* platform during the COVID-19 crisis, because of his experience in creating an atmosphere wherein persons with visual challenges actively participated in his classes on a regular basis.

As the Mental Health Peer Specialist training shifted to online training, the pandemic offered Thomas the support he was lacking to continue in the *Job Readiness Program*. In addition to facilitating the Tai Chi class, Thomas' duties at the SHAC includes tracking members' attendance in the virtual support classes.

On December 27, 2020, Thomas celebrated four years of sobriety with the support of Bruised Apples.

Six months later, in the Summer of 2021, AAMHC supported Thomas in his MHPS training with *Via Hope*. He continues his 250-hour internship under the supervision of The Don Seamster. (Through the *Job Readiness Program,* Austin Area Mental Health Consumers provides a limited number of scholarships each year to attend *Via Hope* MHPS core training as well as the opportunity to earn the required CEU's afterward.)

by debra harman miller 153

We Are the Shac

by debra harman miller

Troy Robert Hawkins 2017

"I first heard about the SHAC through some ears;" said Troy as he started his chapter in the book with a joke.

Actually, he was referred by a counselor. Troy said when he came to the SHAC he was recovering from a gunshot wound to the left side of his head. He signed up for membership his first day. His expectations were that he would find some good people to help him out. For Troy, the SHAC is a very loveable place where volunteers and members would do anything to help each other out.

"I expected to find good people to help me out with stuff. And I found they were very level. They would do anything to help. Thank God, for that."

Troy shares his first reason (to come to the SHAC) was getting a bus pass "because I ride the bus every day from here to there and I stay a long way out north."

Troy loves the guided the meditation and finds it helpful. Incredibly, Troy survived a gunshot to his head in 1993, that left him a paraplegic. He boasts he was shot by a gun, **but he saved the bullet.** As he stands for a photograph, he ads *"But I'm alright today. Thank God for that."*

We Are the Shac

by dEbra harman miller

Virginia Leybas   2020

Hospitality Leader

The *SHAC Snack Program* is more than a soup kitchen, it is an opportunity for advocacy. On the surface, one might think, "Oh, that's nice, they feed the homeless." However, Self-Help and Advocacy has many levels.

It's not what you think....

Applying the vision of the Self-Help & Advocacy Center, as members, we research and encourage independence. As an organization, we meet the consumers' immediate needs with a light meal, while teaching members how to find resources on their own should problems arise again later.

Extensive research and planning is necessary to create programs in response to the needs expressed by members. Pooling information on existing community resources, staff members volunteer their time and resources to pick up donations of ready-to-eat foods five days a week.

After six months, Rita asked Virginia to serve as a volunteer and she was well-prepared for her position as the *Hospitality Leader*. She had worked in the food service industry

We are the Shac

since she was young. Virginia is not only skilled in cooking and preparation, but also in the safe handling and storage of foods. This is even more important as we look at how we can keep our members safe and yet continue the *SHAC Snack Program* while adhering to city guidelines.

Long before she became a member of the SHAC, Virginia had completed her certification and had earned her food handlers' license from the State of Texas. Safe handling begins with logging in food donations and ends after Virginia disinfects the area and makes her report of the number of persons served each day.

Besides preparing, serving the noon meal, and keeping the areas disinfected, Virginia also keeps the coffee flowing and serves sodas, water bottles, and snacks upon demand.

Filling in at the front desk, Virginia has been especially helpful as she is fluent in Spanish and English. Virginia aids in communicating the needs of some members to whom English is a second language.

Steadfast in her commitment to self-care, each weekday Virginia arises before dawn and MetroAccess picks her up at 4:30 am. Taking dialysis would be a full day for most; however, Virginia finds the connection with her peers as the Hospitality Leader energizing. Despite incredibly long days with dialysis and spending four more hours on the bus, Virginia volunteers Tuesday through Friday.

by debra harman miller

Virginia was excited that Capital Area Food Bank held a cooking workshop at the SHAC. The food bank did not just donate the basics to feed a small group of attendees and host a cooking show. She was pleased the food bank representative not only presented information both on community resources to forage for ingredients on a limited budget, but also demonstrated how to handle foods safely. Advocacy empowered the members to not only have lunch that day, but also to have the opportunity to gain skills and information.

As members share their own recipes, the prospect of freedom of choice and self-determination encourages them and leads to better health.

We Are the Shac

by debra harman miller

William Collins   *2017*

William comes to the SHAC on Mondays for the *Bruised Apples {{{SOS}}} Source of Support* group to learn tools to manage his mental health wellness. He shares that the classes led by Don E., LCDC, have really touched his heart.

> *If*
>
> *it wasn't for the*
>
> *Bruised Apples group,*
>
> *I would be kind of lost,*
>
> *because they really*
>
> *help me out a lot.*

We are the Shac

Unlike others, William did not come to the SHAC for a bus pass. His caseworker from ATCIC suggested he try the SHAC after he was injured from a blow to the head from a hatchet.

Long ago, William began self-medicating and abused alcohol to drown out the voices that plagued him. It had been over two months since his last drink and he was trying some twelve-step programs, but he found them lacking in the support he needed for his mental disorder. Despite the opportunities for fellowship, he still felt isolated and found it was hard to open up to others. The *Bruised Apples* group was a welcome supplement to the treatment plan the caseworker at ATCIC prepared for him. New to taking medications for his hallucinations, William was thrilled he was "actually succeeding."

The fellowship at the SHAC gave him a different overview of his problems. As he listens to others share their challenges "it makes me feel kind of like maybe my problems aren't so bad." William feels the respect he receives at the SHAC helps him *to feel like a person.*

They hug me like

I'm a real person!

by debra harman miller

In addition to mental health challenges, William suffers with back problems, especially degenerative disc disease; however, that does not limit his desire to help others. He helps distribute food by volunteering at *Mobile Loaves and Fishes* (a local nonprofit supporting the homeless.) He volunteers at *Pets Alive* (a nonprofit that provides low-cost vaccinations and other veterinary services for pet owners with limited resources.)

He volunteered to assist with the creation of "tent city." (The transitional housing community on the edge of Austin.) William was active in planting the garden before the community opened. As people started moving into the provided housing, William was attacked, and he was offered a place in town instead.

William is grateful for the one-to-one therapy sessions and Social Security benefits that will allow him to focus on his recovery as he learns new job skills. His goal is to return to work and to become independent. He managed to hold on to his previous job for three years, but the hallucinations and paranoia were problematic. Sometimes his boss understood and allowed him to just come in and start working when he was able. These days, William shares his brain is not functioning the same way it did before, and the sedative effects of the new treatment create a struggle.

William
Collins
2018

by *de*bra **har**man **mi**ller

William shares a story about being homeless in Colorado. He had just gotten too tired of struggling, tired of the strains of life. One night he tried to go to sleep and freeze to death but ended up in a coma for ten days instead. Another night, while camping outdoors, he was overwhelmed and had lost hope of things getting any better. He did not want to hurt his children with another botched suicide attempt, so he decided an accident in the woods would be a more noble way to bow out. He knew the bears came through the campgrounds nightly, so he purchased some pastrami and stuffed his pockets with the strong-smelling meat and settled in waiting for the bear to kill him. Waking up in the hospital and not knowing what had happened was a pattern he repeated until he made his way to Texas.

William Collins   *2018*

William has made Austin his home and no longer feels the need to run from the voices he hears. He is connected in his community. He was selected to Advocate for others as a charter member of Homeless Advisory Commission of Austin. HACA was established by the City of Austin to find solutions and resources for the overwhelming influx of new residents. His experience is vital to create change for others who have experienced long-term homelessness. He has always collected what others left as trash and created art; because William sees the beauty in the world around him other people miss. When the Homeless Advisory Commission of Austin, (HACA,) published their 2018 calendar, his insightful piece, aptly named THE STRUGGLE was chosen. William explains it represents your strength through mental health and addiction.

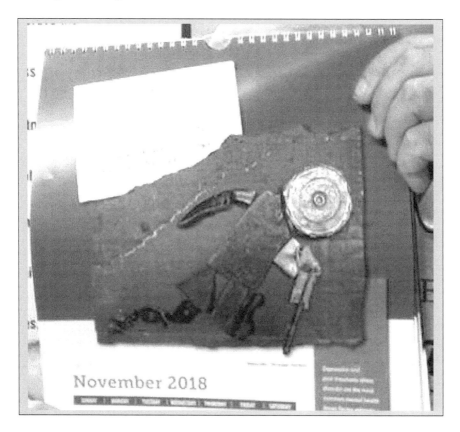

William Collins hoists the HACA calendar and shows the November page revealing his artistic expression of the struggles he faces with substance abuse and mental health recovery.

by debra harman miller

From the Author

debra harman miller

If you or a person you care about suffers with mental or physical challenges; it is my hope that you will share this book with them that they might be released from the prison of terminal uniqueness. Perhaps they are like I used to be... unable to walk or to feed myself due to the permanent side effects of medications prescribed to treat dissociation, such as Parkinsonism or Tardive Dyskinesia?

Ask your caseworker to connect you with a Mental Health Peer Specialist in your area!

*Recovery is **Real** and **Possible** for you, too!*

Her next book, **Play The Tape Thru**©, will be released in 2022.

©Debra Harman Miller – *Stop the Madness Media, Austin, TX, USA*

wearetheshac@gmail.com

We Are the Shac

by debra harman miller